TWAYNE'S WORLD AUTHORS SERIES
A Survey of the World's Literature

SPAIN

EDITORS

Janet W. Díaz, University of North Carolina, Chapel Hill
Gerald E. Wade, Vanderbilt University

Ramiro de Maeztu

TWAS 484

Ramiro de Maeztu

RAMIRO DE MAEZTU

By RICARDO LANDEIRA

The University of Wyoming

TWAYNE PUBLISHERS
A DIVISION OF G. K. HALL & CO., BOSTON

Library of Congress Cataloging in Publication Data

Landeira, Ricardo L
  Ramiro de Maeztu.

  (Twayne's world authors series ; TWAS 484 : Spain)
  Bibliography: p. 147-51
  Includes index.
  1. Maeztu, Ramiro de, 1875-1936. 2. Journalists—Spain—
  Biography.
PN5316.M3L3 1978   070'.92'4 [B]   77-15591
ISBN 0-8057-6325-2

For Pidge

Contents

About the Author

Professor Ricardo Landeira was born in El Ferrol del Caudillo, Spain, but received his university education in the United States. He holds Bachelor's and Master's degrees from Arizona State University, and a Ph.D. from Indiana University with a combined specialization in Spanish and Comparative Literature.

He has taught at Arizona State University and Duke University, was Fulbright Lecturer at the University of Santiago de Compostela, and is presently at the University of Wyoming.

Professor Landeira's areas of specialization are nineteenth- and twentieth-century peninsular Spanish literature. His critical works include *Gabriel Miró: Trilogía de Sigüenza* and the edition, in collaboration, of *Ignacio Aldecoa: Critical Essays*. He has published articles particularly in the areas of ninteenth- and twentieth-century poetry and the novel, these essays appearing in such journals as *Revista Hispánica Moderna, Romance Notes, Boletín de la Real Academia Española, Journal of Spanish Studies: Twentieth Century.* Prominent among several current research projects is a book on José de Espronceda.

Preface

Although Ramiro de Maeztu's name inevitably appears with those of Miguel de Unamuro, Pío Baroja, Ramón del Valle Inclán, Azorín or Antonio Machado, as a member of the literary Generation of 1898, he has not shared his companions' bibliographical affluence. This book is the first such study ever done in English; in Spanish there are only three. Whereas the others' literary output has been graced by several editions of complete works, Maeztu does not even have one. Madrid's Editorial Rialp began in the mid-fifties to publish some of his out-of-print works but gave up after finding the project unprofitable. It was at that point that a second publishing house, Editora Nacional, took over, not only bringing out previously published volumes but also issuing some for the first time, with the intention of doing a complete works series. As of 1974, the centenary of Maeztu's birth, after eight years of no new volumes, it appears that Editora Nacional has decided, instead, to settle for a selected works edition, publishing a handsome tome of the author's best known works entitled *Obra de Ramiro de Maeztu (Ramiro de Maeztu's Works)*. This recent centennial has stirred some critical interest in Maeztu's work; not much, though enough to remind us of his importance in Spain for most of the first thirty-six years of this century as compared to the relative obscurity surrounding him since his death. Two factors account for Maeztu's current lack of appeal among critics—one, purely literary, is his lesser stature as a member of the Generation of 1898 to which he belonged, not on account of his belletristic worthiness (at times denounced), but for ideological ties; the second reason, extraliterary, has to do with his political metamorphosis. The first has a sound basis as can be seen in the study to follow; the second, however, is indefensible from a strictly critical vantage point. The young radical Maeztu became a rabid reactionary, a fascist in the eyes of many. The fact is that, after his death, Franco's dictatorial regime treated his works and his name very kindly, from giving support to special *Festschriften* and other homages to his memory, to bestowing on his heirs the title of "Conde de Maeztu." The anti-intellectual attitude of the dictatorship engendered an indiscriminate disdain on the part of literati for all that Franco espoused. Maeztu and his works have been among the unwitting victims. The imposing volume of his output, together with the unavailability of the greater part of it, the dispersal throughout now defunct journals and newspapers, also plays a large part in some critics' reluctance to undertake a thorough evaluation.

Maeztu was a publicist, diplomat, politician, lecturer, critic, dramatist, and poet, but above all he considered himself a journalist. In his generation as in ours, Spain's greatest authors contributed regularly to the nation's major newspapers. The signatures of Unamuno, Baroja, and Azorín then, Miguel Delibes, Francisco Umbral, and Julián Marías today are well known by people who read only a daily paper. But, unlike them, Maeztu achieved little significance as a creative writer. The one novel, twenty-odd short stories, one play, and the handful of poems he wrote are of negligible literary consequence. Had his production been limited to them, the present study would not be necessary. Maeztu's worth lies instead in the articles, commentaries, and chronicles which he wrote daily for publication in newspapers. Today such an assertion will be received with skepticism, since most readers find in the daily press only information rendered in an objective straightforward fashion, save for the opinion-editorial page. Maeztu's articles were vastly different, however. A journalist of ideas, he interpreted, evaluated, and considered his topics at length. His transcended the circumstances of the subject lending it a theoretical or universal application. In manuscript, these articles were four or five pages long; they are therefore to be recognized as essays where an idea is fully developed along the lines of today's philosophical, sociological, or critical essays, and not merely newspaper articles. He was his generation's most prolific author. The writing of almost forty years, sometimes producing more than one article per day, must have netted Maeztu some fourteen to fifteen thousand essays—a tremendous amount by any standard. And, although such a numerous collection no doubt contains many weak pieces, unfortunately only a fraction have been catalogued or put in book form to this date. He himself published a few books, the ones discussed in the chapters that make up this study, the rest were issued posthumously. All of them, however, are essays previously published in various Spanish, South American, or British periodicals. Some had been done with a book in mind, but published first in a magazine or newspaper for financial and contractual reasons, e.g., *Defensa de la Hispanidad (In Defense of Hispanism)*; others were simply a collection of essays under the criteria of thematic similarity or topical interest, for instance, *Don Quijote, Don Juan y la Celestina*. Sitting down and writing a book constituted for Maeztu journalistic forbidden fruit—he had neither the time, the energy, nor, I suspect, the inclination for it, once his task of fulfilling his daily commitments was over.

Maeztu's period of intellectual importance starts at the end of the Spanish-American War, reaches a high during the First World War, and terminates at the beginning of the Spanish Civil War. It was an existence punctuated by conflict and, to an extent, conditioned by it, especially the last period. In the four months prior to the outbreak of the Civil War, the Republican government could not hold back the bloody chaos that engulfed the whole nation: one hundred and sixty churches put to the torch, two hundred and seventy-one assassinations (mostly political), thousands of cases of personal assault, one hundred and thirteen general strikes and countless partial ones, ten newspaper offices sacked. Tempestuous 1936 saw the disappearance of several of the greatest writers in Spanish literature, some of whom died quietly (Valle Inclán and Unamuno), while others were direct victims of the political hatreds that conjured up the Civil War. Among the first to die at the hands of leftist militiamen in Madrid was Ramiro de Maeztu. Others killed by both sides were Ramiro Ledesma Ramos, Federico García Lorca, Manuel Bueno, Pedro Muñoz Seca, Onésimo Redondo. A few, including Miguel Hernández, died in prison shortly after the conclusion of the war.

In spite of the politicized nature of Maeztu and his work, I have tried to maintain a neutral and objective attitude throughout my commentaries on his texts. My approach has been contextual and as unbiased as is possible under the circumstances. Adhering to the general guidelines of the Twayne series, little effort has been made to produce a work of exclusively original scholarship, of interest solely to specialists on the subject. On the contrary, the aim of this study is to familiarize the average interested reader with Maeztu's work and its place in Spanish literature, while making use of existing criticism, established as sound in its interpretation of the subject. The lack of such an introductory study in English at present dictates its need. Therefore, I have selected for my analyses those works of Maeztu considered by critical consensus as his most important and representative. Unable, due to space constrictions and the unavailability of some of Maeztu's writings, to include a full-length discussion of even all of his collected essays, published as books, I have devoted a major portion of Chapter 7 to the survey of all of his production, fiction as well as nonfiction, in an effort to render a total picture of the man, the writer, his work, and his thought. The translations of all of the titles of Maeztu's works, as well as passages from texts, are my own. They are all free interpretive renderings since my intention is, above all, to convey an accurate meaning rather than the exact stylistic formulation.

RICARDO LANDEIRA

University of Wyoming

Chronology

1874   May 4: Ramiro de Maeztu y Whitney is born in Vitoria.

1881–87   Completes *Bachillerato* studies, Instituto of Vitoria.

1889   Financial reverses plunge the family into bankruptcy.

1890   Maeztu leaves for Paris seeking employment but soon returns, a failure in business.

1891   Goes to Cuba to help with his father's sugar plantation, which is subsequently lost.

1893–94   Maeztu travels through Central and North America. Death of his father (1894). His mother moves the family to Bilbao where she gives private English lessons.

1895–96   First newspaper articles appear in *El Porvenir Vascogado* (Bilbao).

1897   April: Maeztu moves to Madrid and befriends Azorín and Pío Baroja. Briefly uses the pen name of Rotuney, taken from the last letters of his first and last names: RamiRO de MaezTU y WhitNEY.

1898   Spain is defeated in a brief war with the United States. Maeztu enlists as a volunteer for the defense of Mallorca, believed endangered by the American fleet.

1899   Publication of *Hacia otra España (Toward a New Spain)*.

1900–01   April 1: Maeztu begins, under the pseudonym Van Poel Krupp, publication of a serialized novel, *La guerra del Transvaal y los misterios de la Banca de Londres (The Transvaal War and the Mysteries of London's Banks)* in the newspaper *El País*. (Published in book form in 1974).

1901   January: the journal *Juventud* is published by Maeztu, Azorín, and Baroja, surviving for twelve issues. Maeztu reads at the Ateneo his first paper of *Don Quijote* as a work of decadence, loudly rebuffed.

1905   January 4: Maeztu leaves for London, where he will remain for fifteen years, as foreign correspondent for *La Correspondencia de España, Nuevo Mundo, La Prensa*, and other Spanish and South American dailies.

1907   First stay in Germany (June–August) and Holland.

1908   A year of polemics with Ortega y Gasset.

1909   The beginning of a lengthy polemic with Unamuno. Trips to France, Italy and Switzerland.

1914–18   World War I. Maeztu, wearing a British uniform, visits the European fronts. Befriends and comes under the influence of T. E. Hulme.

1916   December 14: marries Alice Mabel Hill. Publication of *Inglaterra en armas (England at War)* and *Authority, Liberty and Function in the Light of War*.

1919   Returns to Spain, settling first in Barcelona and then in Madrid. Begins to write for the newspaper *El Sol* of Madrid. *La crisis del humanismo (The Crisis of Humanism)*, a modified Spanish version of *Authority . . .*, is published.

1923   Beginning of Miguel Primo de Rivera's dictatorship, a regime Maeztu supports.

1924	April–May: trip to fascist Italy; significant probable effects on his political ideas.
1925	June 21: Maeztu teaches in the Middlebury College summer program for three months. Publication of *Don Juan, Don Quijote y la Celestina*.
1927	January 30: forced to resign at liberal *El Sol* due to his ultraconservative editorials.
1927	December: named by Primo de Rivera as Spain's Ambassador to Argentina.
1930	February 19: ceases his diplomatic post with the fall of Primo de Rivera.
1931	December 16: the journal *Acción Española* begins publication with Maeztu as a principal founder. Its inaugural editorial, written by Maeztu, is awarded the "Luca de Tena" journalism prize.
1932	August 10: Maeztu is jailed as a political conspirator, when a rightist uprising by General Sanjurjo fails. Elected to the "Academy of Moral and Political Sciences." His entrance speech was "La función del arte" ("The Function of Art").
1934	Elected Representative to the *Cortes* (Spanish Parliament) from Guipúzcoa. Publishes *Defensa de la Hispanidad (In Defense of Hispanism)*.
1935	Named member of "The Spanish Royal Academy of Language." Maeztu's entrance address was "Sobre la brevedad de la vida en nuestra poesía lírica" ("On Life's Brevity in our [Spanish] Lyric Poetry").
1936	July 31: Maeztu is taken prisoner by leftist militiamen at his friend José Luis Vázquez Dodero's house in Madrid.

1936   August 16: Maeztu's last article during his lifetime appears in *La Prensa* (Buenos Aires).

1936   October 29: shortly after midnight Maeztu is executed at the age of sixty-two.

1947   January 15: the "Ramiro de Maeztu" chair is established at the University of Madrid.

1974   July 18: on the anniversary of the declaration of the Spanish Civil War and Maeztu's birth centenary, Franco honors him by creating the title of "Count of Maeztu" to be bestowed on his children and their descendants.

CHAPTER 1

The Times of War

IN the first months of 1873, Spain was a monarchy in search of a king. Isabel II, daughter of the infamous Fernando VII, had been removed from the throne for her capricious rule and scandalous behavior in 1868. Amadeo of Savoy, a distant relative of the Bourbons and brother of the King of Italy, was then imported by General Prim to fill the vacuum, but he reigned for scarcely one year before abdicating the crown to return to a more peaceful life in his native country. There followed a short-lived Republic, troubled, on the domestic scene, by continuing Carlist warfare and sporadic Federalist rebellions in several provinces. Finally in December 1874, the son of Isabel II (then sixteen years of age) became King Alfonso XII, ruler until 1885.

Madrid, although the nation's capital, was no great city. By day its streets were narrow, badly cobbled and dirty; at night they were ill-lighted by means of oil lamps and even less safe than today. Horse-drawn carriages, water carts, and pedestrians produced the impression of a country village rather than a capital city. Many cafés never closed, offering a meeting place for newspapermen, unemployed office workers, sinecured politicians, and scheming socialists. Life in the provinces, though more tempered, followed proportionately the same rhythm.

I Open Conflict

If domestically these were troubled times for Spain, on the foreign scene the problems were much graver. In Cuba an insurrection begun in 1868 could not be quashed until 1876. That the nation was losing her grip on the reins of power is made obvious by Hugh Thomas' statement that "for many generations Spain had neither been feared as an enemy nor valued as a friend."[1] Again in 1895 guerrilla warfare broke out in Cuba where by December 115,000 Spanish soldiers battled the rebels. In the Philippines, Spain's last colonial war began the following summer. The United States' interventionist foreign policy was renewed by President McKinley during 1897. The Spanish government reacted to Washington's pressure by granting a more liberal constitution not only to Cuba but also to Puerto Rico. Nevertheless, this concession appeased no one. To worsen matters, Cánovas, a popular prime minister, was assassinated on August 18, 1897. His cabinet ruled until a new government could be formed by Sagasta, during whose stewardship the events of 1898 took place.

On February 15, 1898, the United States cruiser *Maine*, stationed off the port of Havana on a courtesy call, inexplicably blew up. Two officers and two hundred sailors died in the holocaust. War was imminent between the two powers; only a spark was needed to ignite the powder keg. The explosion of the *Maine* suddenly provided it. While instructing his Secretary of War to plan for the invasion of Cuba, President McKinley through the U.S. envoy in Madrid made a last offer in the form of an ultimatum to the Sagasta government: Washington would pay Spain the sum of three hundred million dollars for turning Cuba over to the United States, but if Spain refused, the United States would intervene with force. The offer was rejected flatly since, aside from this patently offensive exchange, McKinley had offered one million dollars to each of the Spanish cabinet ministers who aided the negotiations. A further unsuccessful attempt to influence the course of events was made by the president's personal envoy to the Regent María Cristina. The U.S. Senate then introduced a resolution on April 18, 1898, that constituted a declaration of war on Spain.

The United States fleet began hostile maneuvers at dawn on May 1 at Cavite in the Philippines. Under the command of Commodore Dewey the American task force defeated the Spanish contingency directed by Admiral Montojo in a matter of hours. The battle was over before midday. Much the same occurred in the Caribbean theater when Admiral Cervera met his enemy, Commander Sampson, on the morning of July 3. The Spaniards in both cases fought an unequal battle—the old wooden ships proved to be no match for the overpowering steel-hulled U.S. destroyers.

Spain in this short war had lost almost the whole of its navy. Sampson lost one dead and nine wounded in the Cuban action, and

Dewey in the Philippines suffered nine wounded, while Spain, in the naval encounters aside from all the ships lost, had five hundred men killed, another two hundred wounded, with thousands taken prisoner.[2] Many of these, ravaged by tropical diseases, arrived in Spain months afterward, shivering from the cold in their thin tropical outfits, devoured by fever and malnutrition, and depressed by the constant spectacle of the shrouded bodies of those who died en route being thrown into the ocean at hourly intervals.

On August 12, 1898, an initial accord was signed in Washington whereby Spain recognized its defeat and left at the mercy of the United States all of its former colonial overseas territories. On December 8, a delegation from Spain and one from the United States met in France where two days later Spain confirmed internationally, by the Treaty of Paris, her losses of Cuba, Puerto Rico, Guam, the Philippines, and the Mariana Islands to the United States. This treaty signified the end of the Spanish colonial empire. Spain's bankruptcy was total: political, economic, and moral. With the loss of territory came a diminishing of revenues and inexpensive imports such as sugar, tobacco, and coffee. For an economy already weakened by military expenditures, the sudden shakeup was truly serious. The loss of prestige alerted Spaniards to the ineptness of their government, and the immediate future looked very bleak. The cheers upon the inauguration in 1902 of a new king—the ninth in less than a century—had to be extremely hopeful. Ironically, he would be Spain's last monarch for nearly half a century, forced to abandon his own country which soon after his departure would enter into one of the century's cruelest civil wars.

II *The Ideological Panorama*

Joaquín Costa and Francisco Giner de los Ríos are key figures in Spanish intellectual life in the last quarter of the nineteenth century. These two writers were most influential in the education of a new generation of literary men, second in importance only to Spain's Golden Age of letters. Giner's influence on Unamuno, Machado, and Azorín is stronger than on Maeztu who regarded Costa as his teacher and friend. This man was many things: an economist, an engineer, a social scientist, a historian, and a law philosopher. Costa (1844–1911) wanted, perhaps above all else, to raise the standard of living of the rural population. He considered that the best solution was for everyone to have his own piece of land to cultivate. Little by little he came to be regarded as the social spokesman of the period. His motto

"school and pantry" was later adopted by the young Maeztu. Costa
intended government to be strictly an organ of coordination. His low
opinion of the political figures of that time was shared by Maeztu.
Both men resented writers not committed to their cause.

When Costa went to Paris in 1867 to work with the Spanish exhibit
of the World's Fair, Spain's backwardness was so painfully apparent
that he resolved to make every effort to raise his country's level to the
rest of the continent's. When Maeztu later opposed the concept of
Europeanizing Spain to Unamuno's own of Africanizing the penin-
sula, he conceded that it was to Costa whom his generation owed the
vision of Europe as an ideal. Soon after his return from France,
Costa's publications reflected this new resolve, attacking Spain's
indolence, obsession with party politics, preoccupation with past
historical grandeur, and its general disregard for immediate reality.
He pleaded for revitalization through a two-pronged approach
labeled "culture and progress."

Costa's philosophy is best synthesized in the final pages of
Oligarquía y caciquismo (Oligarchy and Bossism), where he argued
for a radical change in the expenditure of funds and national
resources, for the creation of a bureau of change, and reform of the
educational system. He asked for substitution of Spain's traditional
ways by European ones, for the lowering of food prices through
improved methods of agriculture, for more vigorous social legislation
that would better working conditions and bring about social security
in old age. Costa favored a stronger local self-government, making
judicial services available to every citizen, and, finally, he reasoned
that a renovation of all government offices and personnel were
overdue. His great failure was to focus upon social problems only in
the country, eschewing the problems endemic to industry and urban
living. His theories propose a harmonious solution for a rural society
typical of the nineteenth century; he was not living in the present.
When trying to put into action these ideas, by actively participating in
politics, he failed. He did not succeed either in gaining a University
chair but the "Institución Libre de Enseñanza" opened its doors to
Costa, giving him not only a teaching post but also naming him editor
of its journal.

Even if Sanz del Río and later Giner de los Ríos did not have as
great an impact on Maeztu as Costa did, their prestige weighed
heavily upon Spanish intellectuals. Julián Sanz del Río (1814–1869)
was a philosopher and teacher as well as a minor political figure who
felt that Spain had to be shaken out of her intellectual doldrums, and

any social stimulant had to begin at a higher directive and educational level. After his acquaintance with the philosophy of Karl Christian Krause (1781–1832) he applied for and received a grant from the University of Madrid to study abroad, proceeding first to the Sorbonne and thereafter to Heidelberg where he came in contact with Leonhardi and Roeder, both students of Krause. He introduced the teachings of Krause, lecturing and translating the German philosopher's works, from his post as professor of History of Philosophy at the University of Madrid. By introducing this new philosophy in his native country, he awoke not only the interest of many but the animosity of others, especially traditional orthodox Catholics and bureaucrats, because Sanz del Río placed great emphasis on the pedagogical aspects of Krausism and its moral import.

Krause's system is sometimes called Panentheism or harmonious rationalism, an idealistic pantheism recognizing the presence of God as an infinite being in Nature and the finiteness of the world. Although Krausism pretended to be a continuation of Kant's philosophy, it rejected the latter's metaphysical agnosticism. But Krausism in Spain has to be viewed in the light of Sanz del Río's pragmatic thought and its educational implications. The Spanish version of Krausism was not strictly philosophical—it was based on ethics not on metaphysics—but it compounded the literary, religious, and political spheres.

The practical side of Krausism, as interpreted by Sanz del Río, is developed by Francisco Giner de los Ríos (1839–1915). Like Sanz del Río and Costa before him, Giner travelled extensively abroad. As a man of a solid educational background with degrees in philosophy, civil and canon law, music and literature, he was able to compare his nation's inferior status to the rest of Europe. When as a dissatisfied young intellectual he met Sanz del Río in Madrid in 1863, he found in the older man a source of knowledge as well as a kindred spirit. And when Sanz del Río died, Giner became the undisputed head of the Krausist movement in Spain. This thinker felt that genuine social reform must begin with reformation of the individual through education. His political convictions were simple, and can be summarized as the belief that a national government would remain unstable so long as its people did not acquire civic maturity. Giner, then, understood Spain's problem to be one of education, not only of subject matter but also of method—pedagogy—especially the relationship between teacher and pupil. For his times, Giner was an iconoclast. In February of 1875, the Ministry of Education sent a circular to all university presidents to watch out for professors who openly attacked Catholic dogma and national institutions—primarily teachers influenced by Sanz del Río's brand of Krausism. Some were dismissed from their posts—Giner among them—and others voluntarily resigned.

From these two groups that had officially strayed from political and religious orthodoxy, Giner would recruit the "Institutión's" initial faculty. They were not radicals, but their belief that modern man could develop without detectable disadvantage outside of a rigid Catholic existence was anathema to the old guard. During his forced banishment to Cádiz in 1875, Giner decided to work outside the official educational system, creating a private institution for learning. In this period his publishing efforts were considerable—four important books in scarcely two years. Back in Madrid in the following year, he put his project to the test. The "Institución Libre de Enseñanza" had the backing of Spain's liberals and numerous intellectuals. Surprisingly, even a few bankers and members of the bureaucracy, secure in their posts, contributed to the success of the institute, which opened its doors in 1876 under the direction of Laureano Figueroa. Giner was named director in 1881, a post he held in spite of being reinstated to his university chair by the Sagasta government. Spain's intellectual resurgence at the turn of the century must be accorded almost exclusively to the "Institución Libre" and its pedagogues, especially Giner. The Generation of 1898 was deeply indebted to Krausism and the "Institución"—especially for its appreciation of Nature and development of an ethical literature. Its role as catalyst for Spanish intellectual renewal up to and including Ortega y Gasset's work cannot be over-emphasized. If there is a difference between the earlier Krausists and the later ones, closer to the members of the Generation of '98, it is that while the former looked to the future in optimistic terms, the latter saw it more guardedly.

III   The Generation of 1898

The defeat of 1898, a misfortune for Spain, was at the same time a liberation from an imperial dream that consumed her best men and wasted her domestic resources. The date marks the beginning of Spain's contemporary era. Strictly speaking, 1898 has no special literary significance since no single work published that year merits remembering. In broader terms, however, this date symbolizes a literary renaissance, a generation of writers producing a body of literature that rivals in richness Spain's Golden Age of the sixteenth and seventeenth centuries.

The members of this generation (although disagreement still exists among the critics as to its makeup), are Ramón María del Valle Inclán (1866–1936), José Martínez Ruiz, better known as Azorín (1873–1967), Pío Baroja y Nessi (1872–1956), Miguel de Unamuno y Jugo (1864–1936), Antonio Machado (1875–1936), and Ramiro de Maeztu y Whitney (1874–1936). The acrostic ¡VABUMM!, made up from the initials of their last names, is not only a good way to remember them all but constitutes onomatopoeically the impression they sought to convey to their contemporaries—a big bang. Theirs was a rebellious attitude voiced in protests and in their stand against traditional ways of doing—or not doing—things. But the criticism expressed was constructive and their incisiveness was tempered by an anxiety for meaningful reform. The patriotic pessimism of the group caused its members to admire everything European, as Costa and the Krausists had before them.

At the inception of the Generation its closest members, politically speaking, were Unamuno, Azorín, Baroja, and Maeztu. As they matured, all esprit de corps vanished. This happened around 1905[3] although the label Generation of 1898 does not appear until 1913. Azorín used the expression in four articles he wrote that year, when the solidarity of the group had broken down completely, so that its conscious founding strangely coincides with its dissolution. Even though Spain may have ceased to be the essential theme in most of their writings, it remained important for all of them save Maeztu, for whom Spain was the only constant and lasting subject of his entire writings. He and Unamuno possessed the greatest ideological concern, expressed in key essays by both men before 1898. Unamuno's "Sobre el marasmo actual de España" ("On Spain's Present Morass") dates from 1895, Maeztu's "Parálisis progresiva" ("Progressive Paralysis") from 1897. Unamuno was the most protean in his political attitude, Azorín the most subtle, Valle Inclán the most conservative, Baroja the most constant, and Maeztu originally the most radical—his political change constituted a complete about-face.

Azorín, Baroja, and Maeztu published, in December 1901, a document called "Manifesto de los Tres" ("Manifest by Three") offering it as a remedy to Spain's ills. The Three prescribed "the application of scientific knowledge to all social wounds," or, more precisely, "compulsory education, the establishing of agrarian loan offices and the legalization of divorces."[4] Very few people read it, fewer remember it, and no one implemented their suggestions. Their posture echoes the regenerationist theories of Costa, Sanz del Río, Giner, and the Krausists. The small group may well have been the beginning nucleus of the Generation of 1898.

These men were drawn together by a number of factors which, according to Pénder, Petersen, Dilthey, and other theorists of generational studies, constitute a literary generation: coinciding birthdates (all are born within ten years of each other), similar education and upbringing (most were self-educated and considered a library the best possible university), a historical event creating a state of awareness (the disastrous 1898 war with the United States), a common language (Spanish), a common leader (Unamuno and, more remotely, Friedrich Nieztsche), and shared or common experiences (close personal contact in cafés, news-rooms, and meetings). They did their best to distinguish themselves from one another, however, first via attire histrionics: Azorín was seen everywhere wearing a monocle and carrying a red umbrella; Unamuno dressed as a protestant minister; Valle Inclán chose to let his beard fall to his waist and pinned up his coat sleeve in order to make more obvious the loss of that limb; Baroja took to wearing a cap, in part to hide his premature baldness, and a dark overcoat, adopting an unfriendly attitude toward all comers; Machado simply didn't care how he looked and dressed with the grubby carelessness of a poor, rural, high-school teacher; and finally, Maeztu preyed upon others with his thoroughly unpredictable behavior, dressing like an English gentleman but often acting as though possessed by an epileptic fury.[5] This ingenuous clamor for attention soon gave way to a more serious intellectual charge which never lost all its iconoclasm.

Maeztu turned out to be the most prolific of his generation; in forty years of journalism he wrote an average of more than one article or essay per day, which provides a rough idea of the extensiveness of his output. The complete works of approximately fifteen thousand articles would run into the hundreds of volumes. For Maeztu, the newspaper remained his principal organ of expression. Indeed, at that time the newspaper article and mini-essay were the main forms of nonfiction writing. It has been amply documented by recent studies that most political and literary doctrine of the turn of the century is to be found in periodicals. Even today, journalistic articles by Miguel Delibes, Ferlosio, or Cela, Spain's premier novelists, are common. Such pieces dealt and deal preferably with law, sociology, and history as well as literature, and although eschewing erudition, constitute a type of literature characterized by tremendous ideological density. The subject for the Generation of '98 was Spain, which had as its themes Castille as the essential Spain; man in his relationship with God, himself, history, and his country; and a new and possible Spain. Each at one time or another suspected that Spain was the problem and Europe the ideal solution. They early became able journalists but all except Maeztu, who wrote exclusively for periodicals, renounced the press as soon as they could afford it, devoting their energies to the novel, poetry, and playwriting.

IV   *Maeztu, the Others, and Ortega y Gasset*

The personal differences among the members of the Generation of 1898 were many and great. One literary biographer of the period, José María Salaverría, acquainted with all of them, wrote that: "It is true that they respected each other, though they didn't like one another very much. Azorín held Baroja faithfully in high esteem, and that is as far as the congeniality went. Maeztu was jealous of Azorín and detested Baroja. Baroja couldn't stand Unamuno, and Unamuno didn't care for anybody."[6] Baroja, giving a personal and not very objective twist to the events recalled in his *Memorias* (*Memoirs*), says that Maetzu and Azorín once came close to blows, since "Maeztu was always on the verge of provoking conflicts because his claims were so exaggerated that no one could listen to them calmly."[7] Both Baroja and Azorín became oblivious to the political scene as time passed, to the disgust of Maeztu. When Baroja went to London, where Maeztu resided as foreign correspondent, the latter didn't want to see him; Baroja, in turn, came to feel a deep mistrust for Maeztu. The two last saw each other at the end of 1935, when Baroja went to Vitoria in northern Spain. Going he met Unamuno, and on the trip back he chanced upon Maeztu in the same train car. Writes Baroja: "Had I known it, I would have avoided them both and, possibly, they would have done the same with me."[8]

Valle Inclán, whom Maeztu liked, never held any deep feeling for the rest. Unamuno was the writer who most attracted Maeztu but, at the same time, the one who troubled him the most.[9] It is fair to say, however, that he respected Unamuno more than any other member of the Generation. If Maeztu misjudged Unamuno, it was because he was blinded by the latter's strident criticisms of everyone and everything. The charges and counter-charges between Unamuno and Maeztu spread across many newspapers when later they found themselves on opposite sides of the political arena during Primo de Rivera's dictatorship. The most serious exchange resulted when Unamuno labelled Maeztu a lackey of the regime; the latter, in strong language, denounced the egotistic ideology of Unamuno's works. Maeztu was ten years younger than Unamuno and ten years older than José Ortega y Gasset. Maeztu met the future philosopher through José Ortega Munilla, his father and the editor of Madrid's most prestigious daily, *El Imparcial*, where Maeztu collaborated. Like Maeztu's father, Ortega's had been born in Cuba. Initially the relationship between the two authors was that of a big brother, intellectually speaking; Ortega has even been quoted as saying that he owed his inclination toward philosophy to the older Maeztu. But Ortega was not long in rebelling against his former tutor. The polemics began in June of 1908 and developed through a series of articles until October of that year. The argument revolved around the question of men versus ideas, Maeztu contending that the former were superior, while Ortega thought the opposite and went on to prove his point. The exchange demonstrated unequivocally Ortega's intellectual prowess—Maeztu was no match for him and admitted as much in the last article of the quarrel, confessing his inability to distinguish a real antithesis between men and ideas since—rather than being mutually exclusive—they are interdependent. Ortega saw Maeztu as lacking in critical rigor and acumen, and reproached him for his lack of a system of organized thought. Despite this, between 1908 and 1914, friendly references to Maeztu in Ortega's writings are not uncommon and the same is true on Maeztu's part. And in Ortega's first book *Meditaciones del Quijote (Meditations Upon the Quixote)* the dedicatory page reads: "To Ramiro de Maeztu with a fraternal gesture." But, after Primo de Rivera's tenure in office had ended, and the country faced an uncertain political future, on the thirtieth of November, 1930, Ortega published his article "El error Berenguer" ("The Berenguer Mistake") ending it with the exhortation "delenda est monarchia" ("the monarchy must be destroyed"), reminiscent of Cicero's pronouncement at the end of his speeches "delenda est Cartago" ("Carthage must be destroyed"). This infuriated the conservative Màeztu, eliminating any possible future reconciliation. Maeztu felt Ortega had betrayed his own principles, paving the way in intellectual circles for socialist ideas to triumph in Spain. Maeztu died as a result of his vigorous opposition to their establishment.

V   *The Influence of Nieztsche*

The political action of the Generation of 1898 turned out to be totally fruitless. Maeztu was the only one who never abandoned his taste for political action, even if his efforts proved no more successful than those of the rest. Most critics have seen this penchant for political and ultimately social change in the Ninety-eighters as a result of the determining influence of Friedrich Nieztsche (1844–1900). Although the earliest published references to Nieztsche in Spain were made in 1893,[10] Nieztsche's philosophy was spoken of by a select few, and around 1898 known only indirectly, since only a handful could read German. The first translation into Spanish did not appear until 1899. It was probably through a slim study published in France in 1898 by Henri Lichtenberger, *La philosophie de Nieztsche*, that Spanish intellectuals began to learn about Nieztsche. The excitement caused by his ideology, however, was such that by 1905 virtually everything worthwhile of his had been translated into Spanish, beginning with the famous *Also Sprach Zarathustra* in 1899.

As pointed out earlier, a great deal of time was spent by intellectuals in group gatherings in the cafés discussing heatedly, reading from their own writings, and generally speaking out on controversial issues. Maeztu frequented the "Café de Madrid" where the *tertulia* (regular informal gatherings) sessions had been meeting every Wednesday since 1896, including Baroja, Azorín, and a foreigner by the name of Paul Schmitz. A Swiss of German origin, Schmitz was a man of mysterious background who had spent some time in Russia but for three years had been making Madrid his home. It was from him that Maeztu, Azorín, and Baroja learned of Nieztsche. Schmitz needed little encouragement to translate for his Spanish friends from the German text right on the bar table. These improvised translations were the first lessons given the Madrid writers on the new philosophy of the creator of the *Uebermensch*. Unamuno was also curious about the radical foreign current of thought sweeping Europe and, far better educated than the vast majority of his colleagues, decided to look into it on his own. In the end he was not as deeply influenced as his three friends but nevertheless found in Nieztsche ample comfort for his fiercely felt individualism. Unamuno's most profound influences were Kierkegaard and Carlyle.

Gonzalo Sobejano[11] advances the idea that Nieztschean thought offers two sides: a negative view, deeply critical of man, and a positive side which affirms the dawn of a superman. It was this last theory that the young writers ascribed to. In Nieztsche they found that the expressed will to power and the promise of a superman were the most appealing solutions to what they considered Spain's number one problem: *abulia,* or lack of will. Nieztsche gave them a firmness of resolve in which nonbelievers saw destructiveness, arrogance, egotism, heresy, and heartlessness. Nieztschean philosophy served them well. They were intent on revolutionizing Spain's intellectual climate, if not her political ambient, by producing meaningful lasting literature not so much for the present as for the future.

Maeztu felt progressively more apart from fellow members of his generation, especially Unamuno's professed egotism. His ideal is founded on community spirit, the work of togetherness of one generation.[12] Maeztu seldom failed to censure Unamuno's obsession with the monologue—the exaltation of the individual to the detriment of the masses Maeztu considered much more important. There is thus already a pulling away at the bonds of a concerted generational effort. From the initial series of national concerns, the tendency for most of these writers is to retreat to a more isolated stance where one's own position assumes equal importance with the former goal. As he had earlier bridged the divisive issue of Europeanizing versus "Hispanizing" the nation that so troubled Unamuno and Azorín, Maeztu steered a middle course, remaining firm in his resolve to work on his country's behalf. While the rest fulfilled their tasks of teaching, book writing, or lecturing, Maeztu's sole occupation for a greater part of his life continued to be journalism. He alone fully dedicated himself to continuous political, social, and at times even economic, as well as literary, critiques. His essays went beyond the informative or commentary boundaries, to probe and theorize upon derivative larger issues. His social and political awareness rank far above those of his peers.

Literarily, Maeztu is the least stylish and poetic of all the members of the Generation of 1898, due to his almost exclusive cultivation of the essay. Maeztu is no more than an essayist, but he is a good essayist. And yet when in 1898 the publishing of a book meant "an almost unreachable height, painful [and] filled with difficulties; [when just] to get to see one's article in a great newspaper was a triumph in itself" as Azorín[13] wrote, Maeztu's own book *Hacia otra España (Toward a New Spain)* was published simultaneously in Bilbao and Madrid, making him a coequal with Unamuno whose *En torno al casticismo (On Authentic Tradition)* and *Paz en la guerra (Peace in War)* had already made him widely known.

As a result of the widening gap between the members of the Generation, the lesson Maeztu derived from the philosophy of Nieztsche was expectedly, though not radically, different. Maeztu early declared his allegiance without reservations, even boasting about it publicly. As early as 1899, in Bilbao, Maeztu began reading Nieztsche, a habit which probably continued up until 1905 when he left for his post in London. Aside from Lichtenberger's book, which Azorín[14] tells us was passed around from hand to hand, Maeztu had surely read *Thus Spake Zarathustra, The Origin of Tragedy, The Waning of the Idols,* and *The Wagner Cad* among others.[15] It should be quite clear, however, that lacking formal training in this kind of discipline Maeztu could not quite reach Nieztsche's ultimate meaning. Unable to assimilate his thought, Maeztu simply followed him as far as he was able.[16] Azorín, Baroja, and Unamuno, as well as Ortega, have hinted as much.

The former considers that Nieztsche's influence on Maeztu has been exaggerated, that he understood Nieztsche very little, and never professed his doctrine in an integral fashion. What Maeztu usually stands for is authority, Azorín goes on to say, so that if Maeztu praises the superman, it is because such a being represents authority.[17] Azorín thus believes that Maeztu's lasting ideal was one of power and that his interest in Nieztsche was superficial. This is doubtful, for Azorín himself did not envision how well Nieztschean philosophy fit in the course of European life, paving the way for modern authoritarian regimes such as Hitler's Nazi Third Reich, Mussolini's Italy, and Franco's fascist Spain, where Maeztu in his dreams of a new Hispanic imperialism contributed to its initial triumph. Baroja, himself an adept of Nieztsche as well as Schopenhauer, thought that Maeztu wanted to be known as Spain's Nieztsche. Unamuno, who probably understood Nieztsche better than anybody at the time in Spain but who constantly and vehemently denied having even read a book by him,[18] recalled that when he met Maeztu "he was under Nieztsche's power, I believe without knowing him any better than I did, I who have never really known him well and always indirectly."[19] And Ortega, in a more serious vein, declared that both he and Maeztu misinterpreted Nieztsche, among other things, for not taking into account the question of morals.

The sense of his own weak will and that of his fellow Spaniards drove Maeztu to read Nieztsche. The defeat of 1898 made him feel the need for superior men, so it was not for philosophic reasons that Maeztu turned to Nieztsche, but for patriotic ones. In his writings he saw the key to rebuilding a nation from defeat. The utopias that many dreamed of were quickly discarded by Maeztu who understood from Nieztsche that if men were to become superior they had to acknowledge their own weaknesses in order to overcome them. His first public manifestation of Nieztsche's thought is made in the introduction he wrote for the Spanish version of *The Will* by Sudermann, in 1898.

Once it was believed that Nieztsche's influence on Maeztu waned following his departure from Spain in 1905, but in our often-quoted masterful study by Sobejano the error of this theory has been convincingly demonstrated—the presence of Nieztsche in Maeztu's thought, if progressively subtler, is a lasting one. As evidenced in his ideal of a regenerated man, his concern for new values, his positive appraisal of war, his exhortation for a will to power and, through his irrational push to alter his circumstance, Maeztu kept counsel with Nieztsche not only when he first looked for new ideals as a young man, but as a mature war correspondent who saw a salutory effect in the First World War, and finally as a confirmed conservative who sought power on behalf of a Catholic authoritarian Spain. Toward the end of his life, Maeztu withdrew from his former friends: Baroja became a distant figure, Azorín stood alone with his delicate aesthetics. Valle Inclán continued too preoccupied with his literature while growing progressively ill. Unamuno became ever more intransigent and obstinate. And Ortega, who removed the dedication to Maeztu from the second edition of his *Meditations Upon the Quixote*, did not even acknowledge in *Revista de Occidente* the publication of Maeztu's masterpiece *La Defensa de la Hispanidad (In Defense of Hispanism)*.

CHAPTER 2

The Life of Ramiro de Maeztu y Whitney

MAEZTU'S life spans a period of history in which Spain enjoys barely a single decade of continuous peace.[1] His existence is inextricably tied to the time in which he lived. Ortega y Gasset's dictum "I am myself and my circumstance" fittingly applies to Maeztu, a political and social man to the fullest extent of the terms. Was Maeztu true to the original spirit of 1898? Probably more so than the remainder of the members. Yet since the larger number went astray, Maeztu was considered to be the one who deviated when in fact it was Unamuno, Baroja, Azorín, and Valle who chose not to hold to daily confrontations with the government and the national tide from the pages of news dailies and magazines.

I The Early Years

Ramiro de Maeztu y Whitney was born in Vitoria, capital of the Basque province of Alava, on May 4, 1874, two days after the Carlists abandoned the nine-month siege of Bilbao under the agreement between monarchists and liberals called the Truce of Vergara. This time is recalled by Unamuno in his first novel, *Peace in War* of 1897. Ramiro was the eldest of the five children reared by Manuel de Maeztu, a Cuban-born Basque, and Joan Whitney, daughter of the British consul in Paris. The father was a strict disciplinarian who exerted a great deal of influence and authority over the young child, subjecting him to a physically and morally regimented life: "My poor father would tell me ever since my early years that I had to be a gentleman, an athlete and a scholar."[2] The results of this firm guiding hand were excellent as young Ramiro's high school (1882–1888) records attest, especially in his preferred subjects, history and rhetoric. From his mother he learned to speak English with native

31

facility. It is not likely, however, that he ever mastered the ancient Basque language. His childhood and adolescent periods were normal ones. If Ramiro had any advantage, it was his father's inherited wealth, a sugar plantation in Cuba which permitted private tutors, riding lessons, and other beneficial pastimes. But these capitalistic remains of his grandfather's estate were soon to be lost. In 1889, at the age of fifteen, Ramiro's formal education was interrupted. Money had run out. Fearing total bankruptcy the elder Maeztu journeyed to Cuba to remedy a pressing economic situation. Don Manuel hoped to send word to his wife that the pawned home furnishings, the lost servants, and dismissed tutors had only been a bad dream. Ramiro was sent to Paris by his mother to learn a profession that would enable him to earn a living. In the French capital he stayed at the home of distant relatives who introduced him to a successful businessman. After a few months, however, the sixteen-year-old apprentice was dismissed by his employer for lack of aptitude. The awaited letter from Cuba never came and, having sufficiently recovered from his recent failure in Paris, Ramiro decided to go to his father's aid. In 1891, he embarked on the trip across the Atlantic.

The sugar plantation "El Pelayo" no longer belonged to the Maeztus by the time Ramiro arrived in Cuba. For a time he worked as a field hand with his father doing menial labor to regain the lost properties. In the end, his pushing bread carts at 6 A.M. through the streets of Havana[3] did little to stave off the inevitable. The economic floundering had been the result of activities in favor of independence from Spain. In this situation of conflict Ramiro learned much regarding the colonial troubles that ultimately proved to be forerunners of the revolution and war of 1898. He gained first-hand knowledge of the corruption and governmental mismanagement of Spain in ruling Cuba.[4] Aside from a political and social awakening, Ramiro became intimately acquainted with labor and economic practices. Seeking more remunerative work, he left the plantation and found employment in a tobacco factory in Havana. Here, while workers hand-rolled the famous cigars, Ramiro, standing on a platform, would read aloud from novels and books of his own choosing. For four hours a day he entertained and educated those laboring below with works by Galdós, Kipling, Ibsen, Marx, Kropotkin, and Schopenhauer. This was the future author's first profitable contact with literature.

As the only break from his duties in four years, Ramiro visited New York just before his twentieth birthday, a two-week stay at the end of

1893 to which no subsequent reference is made. But the impression must have been favorable, since he returned to the United States some thirty years later for a considerably longer period. The hard physical labor and the tropical climate of the Caribbean island began to take a toll on his health, and when a letter from his mother asked him to return to help with the problems of four growing brothers and sisters, Ramiro welcomed the opportunity. A few months later, the family received notice of don Manuel's death in Cuba. This painful chapter thus closed forever, the mother and five children moved to Bilbao. There Joan Whitney opened a small school, where she taught English to children of the upper-class industrialists.

The four years spent in Cuba were decisive for the character of Ramiro de Maeztu. Living and toiling among people who hated his own country drove him to think for himself, to weigh and consider what he saw, and try and synthesize it to derive some sense from it. Because the judgments made were his own, they often seem coarse and radical. But because these arguments were arrived at so personally, Maeztu defended them jealously. In spite of these shortcomings, Maeztu had a tremendous advantage over his fellow writers—his sources were his own experiences, derived from the long stay overseas. Though probably unpleasant for a young man accustomed to study and leisure for most of his life, these proved invaluable in Maeztu's long apprenticeship in politics, literature, and economics. The choice of entering the university was not open to him as it was to Unamuno, Baroja, and the rest—with the exception of Valle Inclán who, together with Maeztu, was the only other member of the Generation of 1898 to see the New World.

II *The Start of a Lifelong Career*

In Bilbao in 1895, Maeztu's career as a journalist began when he was barely twenty-one years old. He went to work at the offices of *El Porvenir Vascongado,* a local paper, translating telegrams and dispatches from English wire services until he was able to convince the editor that his ability to write equalled his ambition to succeed at it. His first article dealing with the war in Cuba turned out to be quite successful: it was carried by the national press and praised for its obvious first-hand knowledge and fresh information. Subsequent articles were equally well received, and Maeztu began seriously thinking of journalism as a permanent occupation. He remained in Bilbao for another two years, increasingly dedicated to his work in *El Porvenir Vascongado.* Yet Maeztu found that he could not separate

his life from his work, that the controversies raised by his articles on
the Cuban conflict spilled over to his political arguments in the city's
cafés and bars. The local army bosses, who did not at all like his
ideological stance nor his incisive pieces which shed so much light
and blame on them, sought an opportunity to have him silenced.
Maeztu had not been called to military duty when he became eligible
because, thanks to the lottery system, he had been able to avoid it.
But through some manipulation the local draft board reversed itself
and put Maeztu into uniform. The first thing the military did was to
put him in prison. After much arm twisting on the part of his mother's
influential friends, charges against him were dropped, and the draft
board was persuaded to reverse itself once more. Ramiro was
extradited to Madrid where, ironically, his future lay. Also, perhaps
in regret at not having served his country in the military, the young
man did a brief stint with the Spanish Army from April to August of
1898 "defending" the island of Majorca from a possible invasion by
the U.S. Sixth Fleet when anxiety was high pitched during Spain's
confrontation with the United States.

At this stage Maeztu was characterized as disagreeable, unconge-
nial, and totally humorless. In his early twenties he was a tall, clean
shaven, dark haired man who possessed a deep and grave voice that
he knew how to use to his advantage. These attributes and his
sensationalistic attitudes, together with his own rebellious version of
Nietzschean philosophy, made the young Maeztu the *enfant terrible*
of the Generation of 1898.

Once in Madrid, Maeztu resumed his café and newsroom routine.
The *tertulia* which he initially frequented was that of the future
Nobel playwright Jacinto Benavente who encouraged and gave him
access to *Germinal*, the first Madrid journal where Maeztu published
poetry and short stories. This helping hand was all he needed, and
soon his articles began to appear in *El Imparcial*, much to the envy of
the members of his generation. He no longer wrote fiction in the
columns of Madrid's papers, but instead took up where he had left off
in *El Porvenir Vascongado*. Mediocre politicians, inefficient institutions, anacronistic ideals, and rhetorical values all became targets of
his revisionist campaign waged between 1898 and 1905, the year he
left Madrid for England. According to Baroja,[5] Maeztu's temerity
forced him to leave the country. It seems that in one of their endless
café gatherings, Valle Inclán and others ridiculed the editor of
Revista Nueva. A couple of weeks later an account of the session in
Madrid Cómico placed all the blame on Valle Inclán. So acerbic was
the piece that upon running into the responsible journalist two nights

later, Maeztu broke the cane he was carrying on the other fellow's head. Baroja—a trained physician—claimed that the wounds were serious enough for the injured man to spend the better part of a month bedridden. Maeztu stood trial and, rather than wait for an unfavorable sentence to be handed down, took the next boat to London. Though undeniably entertaining, and at least partially credible, Maeztu's possession of a prior contract to *La Correspondencia de España* appears closer to the truth than Baroja's account. At any rate, the year and change of locale mark the second stage of Maeztu's career.

III   *The Foreign Correspondent in London*

Although when he left in January of 1905, Maeztu went as the foreign correspondent to the Madrid paper, soon after his arrival in the British capital he also took on the same job for *La Prensa* of Buenos Aires. Up to his assignment in London, Spain had foreign correspondents only in Paris to pick up international news beyond its borders. It thereafter became necessary for every ambitious publisher to have a roving reporter abroad or else one in London as well as in Paris.

Going to London was probably—in Maeztu's own words—the most important event of his life. From his fifteen-year stay abroad (1905–1919), he gained a new perspective on Spain through an enlarged horizon; there he married, and his only son was born. Strangely enough, and in spite of an English mother, wife, and son, Maeztu did not become as anglicized as one might assume.[6] This may be due to intensely close ties with his cultural background: he went back to Spain frequently, he wrote daily in Spanish at least one newspaper column and sometimes several, and even though his readings were not often in his native language, they were all directed to his country's interests.

Living in London did change his day to day routine for the better; in Madrid it had been the atmosphere of the café alternating with the newsroom almost to the exclusion of his rented room, used only for sleeping. This bohemian existence, lacking in organization, schedules, or plan ceased to exist when he rented an apartment on Brenwill Street off Brunswick Square. The more urbane behavior of Londoners, the initial sense of insecurity felt as a foreigner in a country with a totally different language, customs, history, and a more successful present gave Maeztu pause to think. His routine became more orderly also because he was more alone. Gone were the days when dawn would send him home from the animated nightly *tertulia*. "He [now] would get up early, [to] study philosophy and Greek, read the European dailies and write his articles. He worked ten hours a day."[7] In the context of this personal and intellectual order, Maeztu sent to the Spanish press few news items; his chronicles were rather a continuous commentary on the English way of life and thought.

He complained of his solitude in a letter to Rubén Darío: "I have lived for eight years [it was then 1913] in London the most solitary and boring existence invented by civilization.... There have been times when I've spent up to seven weeks without any other human relation than the waiter's at the restaurant where I customarily eat my meals."[8] His gregariousness impelled Maeztu to seek an active intellectual climate in which he could listen and discuss his new-found ambient. He not only continued to send dispatches to the Spanish papers, but also collaborated in several British journals, among them the weekly *The New Age*, where H. G. Wells and Somerset Maugham published their socialist essays. His attraction for Socialism at this time drew him also to London's Fabian Society and brought him into contact with such people as the Russian Kropotkin, father of his country's Socialism and then a refugee in London.

Maeztu developed a liking for travel which he could easily afford as a successful foreign correspondent, the highest paid "literary" occupation in those days. Between trips to Spain, he went in 1907 to The Hague, Kiel, Holland, and Germany. During 1909 and 1910, he again visited Paris, staying for some time in Italy. These impressions of travel are collected in his daily commentaries, often evincing disappointment with his country as a result of the intellectual, technical, and material superiority observed everywhere he travelled. Spain remained for him, even in this voluntary exile, the focal point of his highest ambitions. At first humiliated by the obvious superior levels of other European capitals,[9] Maeztu even wondered if the Anglo-Saxon race was not above his own.[10] The admiration for these centers and their initial fascination began to wear off with experience, as Maeztu realized that each system had its own endemic weaknesses and that, very possibly, neither England's nor Europe's ways were right for Spain whose most serious deficiencies were an absence of "loyalty to any supraindividual values."[11] Thus began the disillusionment that ended in an acute ideological crisis and radical change in his spiritual life. His stay in England, like Ortega's in Germany, did much to help open Spain's eyes to Europe.

In a better spiritual situation, Maeztu began to fill out his intellectual education. Modern ideological currents fascinated him, and in order to gain a more solid knowledge, he decided to go to the source—Germany. First in 1911 and again in 1913 he travelled to Marburg, the center of neo-Kantian philosophy where Cohen and Hartmann each quarreled with the other's interpretation of the master of German Idealism. It was with the two disciples of Kant that Maeztu studied, coinciding there once again with Ortega. Cohen's seminars on metaphysics no doubt advanced Maeztu's philosophical training to a high degree, but here again, as with Nietzsche, it is debatable how much he was able fully to appreciate. It certainly was enough to steer him back to the practice of his childhood beliefs.[12]

Kant—"the firm basis for my religious training"[13]—confirmed for him the existence of the soul or spirit, teaching him that this spirit can derive only from another spirit and not evolve from an inferior thing such as matter. To find such affirmation in Kant meant for Maeztu a decided break with the dicta of materialism so tempting in the past. According to Tierno Galván's study of his thought, Maeztu then readily admitted the religious concept[14] of dualism and the existence of the eternal. "The three fundamental truths of the conception of the world to which Maeztu definitely adhered were, the spirit, nature, and God. On the one hand, from the synthetic a priori judgments he draws the conclusions leading to the eternal that, with the teleological sense that Maeztu gives them, Kant himself had repudiated, criticizing the proofs for the existence of God."[15] Maeztu began with Kant but went beyond him, perhaps thinking that the philosopher's denial of an intellectually verifiable proof of the existence of God in his *Critique of Pure Reason* needed to be pushed aside. The lesson, drawn from the *Critique of Practical Reason*, was that even though it cannot be proven that God exists, the need for that existence, its desirability, is demonstrable since man's behavior should be the same as if He did exist. Maeztu's new-found religious and philosophical fervor was such that upon his return to London he instituted a weekly meeting at his apartment with readings from Kant and Cohen's lectures commented upon by everyone, with Maeztu himself translating directly from the German texts.

IV   *World War I and the Changes Wrought*

The next time Maeztu returned to Germany was in 1914, wearing the World War I uniform of a British war correspondent. When the conflict broke out the second of August, he was in Madrid. Rushing to

London, he had himself assigned to the press corps and then shared the trenches throughout Europe with the rest of the British troops. Flanders, Italy, and France were his longest stays; from there he sent accounts which inevitably found a space in the front page of more and more Spanish language newspapers.

With the advent of World War I, the admirable qualities Maeztu had envisioned in the Anglo-Saxons proved to be simply a mirage. England, Germany, and the rest of Europe could not serve as examples for Spain if they sought to annihilate one another through total war.[16] These war years became another turning point in Maeztu's mind. Spain, regarded as inferior to these nations now wreaking havoc with the very stability of civilization, suddenly merited a second look.

The result of the world conflict on Maeztu's ideology was no less significant. It was an absolute and, from a religiously orthodox point of view, positive change. Its root went back a few years before the beginning of the war when Maeztu met a disciple of the French syndicalist and fascist George Sorel. The man's name was T.[homas] E.[rnest] Hulme. Born in 1883, Hulme had in the early part of his life worked his way through Canada in farms and lumber camps, travelled to Belgium, Italy, Germany, and other European nations that Maeztu had also visited, and when they met around 1911, a friendship was soon struck. Hulme's house, at 67 Frith Street in London, served as a gathering place for weekly discussions on ethics and philosophy by Middleton, Gandier, Ezra Pound, and Epstein, and others. Hulme, a great enthusiast of ethical doctrines, did not care for the relativism modern thinkers lent to the question of Good and Evil. Hulme was not an original philosopher but an impatient thinker who had no use for hypocrisy or vague metaphysics. He possessed a great sensitivity for ideas and the realm of art which he interpreted with arguments often borrowed from Sorel, Bergson, or Pascal.[17] This man remained relatively obscure as a thinker; his main work, *Speculations*, remained unpublished until seven years after his death in 1924. It was without a doubt "his fearless individualism"[18] which attracted Maeztu to him, a man with a strong faith in himself. They met at a lecture Hulme gave in Cambridge in which he spoke about the Romantic notion of the denial of original sin and the resulting view that man was therefore a king in chains. Hulme and subsequently Maeztu took the opposite stand, attacking not only Romanticism but any utopian notion. Hulme's religious influence on Maeztu was not only dialectic but physically palpable too. When the

World War broke out, Hulme joined an artillery company but found nothing romantic once in the midst of the conflict. Nonetheless, wounded and sent to a rearguard hospital, he again volunteered, only to be killed during a shelling of the trenches on September 28, 1917.

Suffering and death confronted Maeztu as well, yet the example set by Hulme (that the weakness of the flesh can be overcome through a strong commitment to duty and that valor can be found if one thinks of the common good) was for the former a revelation. Hulme did not like the war yet he defended it in a series of articles—"War Notes"— written behind the lines, because of the consequences he foresaw if Germany won. Aside from the transcendency of the doctrine of original sin which started the iconoclast on the road back to Catholicism, Hulme taught Maeztu that there is no finality except in religion, which has as its principal object a persuading notion that man must recognize his own limitations, an explanation of why he fails in his highest goals and endeavors. Man's failure is thus intrinsic to his nature. This religious view, utterly pessimistic, may conform to stoicism but not necessarily to Christian orthodoxy, which, while persuading man to recognize his own imperfections, at the same time extends the hope of faith and ultimate regeneration through Christ's Redemption. However, it was enough for Maeztu, who needed only the initial push to return to the course abandoned in his youth. This increase in Maeztu's religious inclination has been repeatedly mislabeled as his "conversion." Brought up as a Catholic, he always considered himself as one. No attack can be found in his aggressive journalism against the Church. If he had strayed away, it was because as an intellectual he did not feel the Church, as an institution, offered any remedies for the ills of his nation.

V   *The Return to Spain*

Two events mark the year 1916 as one of the most important in Maeztu's intellectual and private life: the publication of *Authority, Liberty and Function in the Light of War*, testifying to his spiritual crisis, and the end of his bachelorhood of forty-two years. The marriage to Alice M. Hill took place in Saint Francis Church in London on December 14, 1916, and was officiated at by a Basque priest, Fr. Elizondo, who had gone to England to purchase books unavailable in Spain.[19] An only child, Juan Manuel, born to the couple in London, works today as an officer in the special services branch—translator—of the Spanish Army.

After World War I Maeztu grew more and more disenchanted and decided to end his fifteen-year exile. Possibly other reasons compelled him to return: his advancing age (nearly fifty); his son, who according to a friend, [20] could hardly speak Spanish; and his desire to participate more directly in Spain's affairs.

He had changed markedly from the angry rebel of 1905. Returning after the Peace of Versailles in 1919, Maeztu enjoyed a considerable reputation not only in his own country but in England and South America. This last stage of his life is more intense, productive, rewarding, and tragic than either the time spent in Cuba or in London. Maeztu, at his peak and determined to halt Spain's backsliding, insisted on making his ideas count. Even his friendly antagonist, Miguel de Unamuno, decided to run for Congress on the Republican ticket in 1919. The situation called for it.

The Maeztu family arrived in Barcelona, remaining briefly. Here Maeztu joined Eugenio D'Ors, Corominas, and Gabriel Miró, resting and talking about his experiences in England. [21] Miró left for Madrid in July of 1920 and Maeztu soon followed, settling there once again. His principal occupation was writing a two-column article for *El Sol,* an editorialized commentary dealing with anything and everything. Directed by Manuel Aznar, the paper was openly leftist, making Maeztu's feature very prominent with his right-wing views. His first piece dates from November 17, 1920, in Geneva where he journeyed to cover a meeting of the League of Nations.

His prestige was such that most offers to lecture and contribute articles could not be accepted. Yet when the opportunity to teach in a U.S. institution presented itself, he did not want to turn it down; there was too much to see in this country. Maeztu came to Middlebury College for the summer session of 1925, lecturing on broad topics of Hispanic culture: the literary figures of Don Quijote, Don Juan, Celestina, and the paintings of Velázquez, Goya, and El Greco. During the three months in Vermont, he visited a number of places on the East Coast (what dazzled him most were New York's skyscrapers). He reacted enthusiastically to the industrial and technological advances of a healthy capitalistic society, mentally noting improvements his own country could benefit from. His experiences in the United States, as evinced by daily articles sent to *El Sol,* were rather enjoyable.

Back in Madrid, Maeztu renewed his analysis of the local political scene with the added perspective afforded by his stay in the United States. He considered New York and Moscow two opposite poles of the modern world. His hard-line attitude led him to condemn the

Russian capital, closely coinciding with the political ideals of a powerful and popular military figure of the time, General Miguel Primo de Rivera. Except for Maeztu's lone voice, *El Sol* did not approve of a more authoritarian government than that of the playboy king Alfonso XIII, but other newspapers (the right-wing *Informaciones,* the monarchist *ABC* and even moderates like *El Debate*) had been for some time calling for a dictatorship. In 1923, in a bloodless coup d'etat, Primo de Rivera came to power almost by popular demand. Maeztu's political thought by that time was already more reactionary. It was only natural that his anti-communist warnings—later anti-republican—should have been welcomed by the dictatorship with which he soon openly sympathized. However, even if the majority supported Primo de Rivera, the country's intelligentsia were largely against him. Though Maeztu's intellectual esteem remained high, the closer he attached himself to the regime the more separated he was made to feel from his former colleagues. A campaign either to draw him away from the dictatorship or silence him culminated in 1927 when, his conservative stance in *El Sol* having become morally untenable, Maeztu handed in his resignation. *La Nación* of Buenos Aires immediately offered him a space for his column, and he accepted willingly.

Maeztu, torn by the uncertainty of the political scene, deplored the lack of a popular input into government, yet at the same time observed with what complacency Spaniards lived without care for voting or manifesting constructive desires. Maeztu's halfhearted support of Primo de Rivera became complete advocacy of his approach. Maeztu suspected that his fellow citizens would not bother to vote, or else would play into the hands of local political chieftains and powerful interest groups, bringing about a government less desirable than the dictatorship. Maeztu recognized the perils in such a system of government but opted for it, convinced that it was the only way to rescue the country from the anarchy of the previous decade (1917–1923) when, in less than six years, twelve governments had failed and important Church and State leaders had been assassinated. So, for the first time in his life, Maeztu joined a political party—Primo de Rivera's Unión Patriótica. Thus identified with the regime, Maeztu was hard pressed to keep an objective stance that would enable him to disagree with the official line. In January 1927, the king presented Maeztu with the Great Cross of Alfonso XIII, an honor that the writer's enemies wasted no time in turning against him.

Secure in his political convictions and his economical status as chief correspondent for *La Nación*, Maeztu began writing a series of articles which clearly detailed his growing reactionary ideology. Gone is the moderate tone and controlled expression previously used so convincingly. He sounded more like Primo de Rivera himself, and reward was not long in coming. In December, 1927, Maeztu was named Spain's ambassador to Argentina, where his name, as a contributor to both of its major newspapers *La Prensa* and *La Nación*, was well known. As is usual with political appointments, Maeztu had never been to the country assigned. But his other qualifications for the post were unquestionable; the usual problems of language, knowledge of the host country's heritage and present status did not exist in Maeztu's case. His fifteen-year stint as international correspondent provided him with a skeptical view of world politics, and he was very much aware of what awaited him. From a passive role as a witness of history's making, he had been thrust into an active one. Journalism was abandoned for the duration of his diplomatic assignment. He had earlier declined the post of Minister of Education as well as the directorship of *La Nación* in favor of remaining a journalist so that the final choice was not easy.

His ambassadorship, coinciding with the progressive presidency of Argentina's Irigoyen, was uneventful. In Buenos Aires, he enjoyed his role as Spain's representative. He discharged his diplomatic duties giving numerous speeches, some of which in retrospect proved to be significant in Maeztu's own career, such as the series on the *Quijote*, by lending his journalistic expertise in publishing ventures like the weekly *La Nueva República*, and by introducing visiting Spanish dignitaries and other personalities to Argentinians. The sole exception was the lecture tour by Ortega y Gasset. It is doubtful that the two former friends—by then declared enemies— talked or even saw each other. Maeztu left Argentina February 19, 1930. His end as an ambassador came when the dictatorship fell, even though it was suggested both by the king and his new Secretary of State, the Duke of Alba, that Maeztu continue as his country's representative. He came away having gained a new insight into Spain's historical triumphs, having been able to apprehend the meaning that the discovery, conquest, and colonization of South America had for its inhabitants. This appreciation gave rise to his later ideal of "Hispanidad," a Pan-Hispanicism based on the common heritage of the Spanish-speaking world.

Following the voluntary retirement of Primo de Rivera and his subsequent self-exile to France, Spain found herself in a chaotic situation similar to the year 1923 when the dictator came to power. The vacuum was filled with social, religious, and political turmoil whose pitch increased by the week. Maeztu, a firm believer in order and progress, remained convinced that without a firm hand at the helm there was no way to end the national unrest. A popular democratic government would, in Maeztu's mind, further weaken the nation through its slow operation, whereas an authoritarian regime ruling by decree could stop Spain's disastrous course. Having survived World War I, he felt it better to live under an authoritarian government which could not only protect its people but also control them. This time, however, a Republic came into being in 1931, Spain's second and last in this century. Black clouds gathered over the nation unleashing a death-dealing storm which climaxed in one of the most devastating civil wars the world has ever seen.

VI   *The Role of Fascism*

Fascist ideology played a key role in the Spanish Civil War, and Maeztu was one of its most prominent theorists.[22] Another journalist, however, Giménez Cabellero, a raging socialist, introduced fascism in Spain. He had known Benito Mussolini and Curzio Malaparte in Italy during Primo de Rivera's term in office and upon his return in 1928 offered a vociferous apology for a movement of religious and political militancy. Another extremist, Ramiro Ledesma Miranda, an early admirer of the Nazis, drew up his own program, copying Hitler's military state, which attracted a number of followers, among them Onésimo Redondo who had had a first-hand look at the Nazis in action. These two reactionaries formed the "Juntas de Ofensiva Nacional- Sindicalista" (la J.O.N.S.) in 1931, which had as its basis the support of a militaristic Catholic regime. José Antonio Primo de Rivera, son of the fallen dictator, cut the most dashing figure of the fascist movement in Spain and was one of its first victims. An ardent monarchist and devout Catholic, he wasted no time seeking and carrying out the most expeditious solution. He admired both Hitler and Mussolini for their total commitment to an elitist state. The party he founded became in Franco's Spain the only officially sanctioned political body. Named the "Falange Española" in 1933, it sub-sequently joined with the J.O.N.S., and José Antonio was recognized as leader of the united party. These four men saw civilization on the one hand and communism, or Bolshevism, on the other. The methods employed by a fascist regime (which substituted religion for race, thus distinguishing it from Nazism), seemed to them the best way to remain safe from Russia's threat.

Maeztu, who after his return from Argentina had renewed his journalistic career in newspapers of Spain and Argentina, dropped earlier commitments to write for archconservative dailies such as the monarchist *ABC*. Maeztu sought the company of kindred ideological souls with whom he founded a society in December of 1931 called "Acción Española." The organ of the newly formed fraternity was a magazine of the same name first published at the end of 1931. The inaugural issue contained a long editorial by Maeztu himself which later received the coveted "Luca de Tena" literary prize for that year. Even though he lived off his writing, Maeztu drew no money for his constant contributions to *Acción Española* nor for his work as the society's president. The undertaking was financed by wealthy members of the establishment who liked the group's counter-revolutionary philosophy. Both the Marquis de Quintanar and the Marquis de Pelayo became generous Maecenas.

Acción Española was Maeztu's journal; its objectives coincided with his own, and here he published a great deal of his later books. Its format was stark and produced the impression of a document or thesis paper rather than a magazine. It did not sell very well, since Madrid was a cosmopolitan city and *Acción Española* was not even remotely fashionable; still it survived longer than most periodical publications born out of a narrow ideological group. It did aspire to reach a large number of readers, including Latin Americans also disenchanted with the United States' imperialism. *Acción Española* advocated instead Maeztu's own brand of political philosophy which he called "Hispanidad" (Hispanism). The failure of a monarchist uprising on August 10, 1932, by General Sanjurjo marked the first shutdown of the magazine. All the members of its editorial board were jailed for preaching "an absolutist imperialism." Maeztu was taken into custody in Bilbao and then transferred to a Madrid prison where he spent several weeks.

VII *The End of a Political Order and Maeztu's Own Demise*

The Left totally dominated the Second Republic, then in power. Trade unions, Marxists, socialists, Trotskyites, and even anarchists and separatists occupied every seat of government. No right wing existed for several reasons: the conservatives were outnumbered, poorly organized, and harbored mistrust among themselves, especially of their intellectuals. Maeztu was hated by the leftists and looked upon with suspicion by the Right for his intellectual forth-rightness. The low key position of the conservatives or nationalists meant that, if present conditions prevailed, the country could only move in one direction—further left. The Republicans' greatest error was their extremism. The explosion that Maeztu had forecast for so many years was now at hand. The looting of convents, burning of churches, politically-motivated imprisonments, closing down of newspapers, dismissals from civil service jobs, confiscation of private property without compensation, murder, and other abuses caused a vast number to seek political asylum abroad. Some were the very ones who had done so much to bring about the Second Republic, among them Pérez de Ayala and Ortega y Gasset.[23] From exile, they denounced the atrocities.

Maeztu, living the last four years of his life, continued amid all these alarms to work on behalf of nationalism, social justice, and authority in government with a principal objective of defeating the revolution. For this he was rewarded by the Academy of Moral and Political Sciences which elected him to membership in 1932. His inaugural speech on "The Purpose of Art" reaffirmed his ethical criterion against a merely aesthetic concept of art. In 1934, Maeztu left Spain to travel through Europe for the last time. France, Belgium, and Germany detained him longest. From Germany he brought back praise for the principle of a national ideal and Hitler's achievements, although he criticized severely the racist policies which he did not feel were essential to Nazism.[24] That same year he was elected to Spain's House of Representatives (Cortes) by the Basque province of Guipúzcoa. Maeztu's finest hour came when on June 30, 1935, he read his entrance speech as the Spanish Royal Academy of Letters' newest member. "The Brevity of Life in Our [Spanish] Lyric Poetry," a study of the poetic theme of the passage of time in literature, was also to be his literary farewell to the world of letters.

In the elections held on February 16, 1936, the leftist coalition "Popular Front" won a victory at the polls. Maeztu's name appeared on several political blacklists across the country, but even so he kept up his writing (under the pseudonym "Cualquiera" in *La Epoca*) and speech-making, sowing counterrevolutionary ideas. At that time he resided on Espalter Street in Madrid, a city where he must have known that human life was expendable and his own rested in the hands of a growing number of enemies. Nearly 100,000 persons were executed or assassinated between January and September of that year, the Republican government intermittently appearing wont to interfere with the illegal killings.[25] María de Maeztu advised her brother to flee to southern France but he refused to leave Madrid. Finally in the days prior to July 18, Maeztu gave in and went to stay with José Luis Vázquez Dodero. This friend, a former staff member of *Acción Española*, witnessed Maeztu's incarceration on July 30. Both were taken into custody by a small group of militiamen and led to the Women's Model Prison on Marqués de Mondéjar Street. Although the two men were told they would be shot that very afternoon, months passed uneventfully. Communist papers publicized Maeztu's imprisonment, an event that did not go unnoticed in other dailies but which received no editorial comment from friendly publications such as *La Prensa* of Buenos Aires where he had collaborated for some thirty years.[26]

The British Foreign Office and its Embassy in Madrid did little to save Maeztu, the son of an Englishwoman, married to a British subject, who had spent fifteen years in London, producing two highly laudatory books about England and had worn a British uniform as a war correspondent in World War I. Britain's Embassy, powerful and influential, did nothing because Maeztu was on the "wrong side" according to the English. His wife and young son were granted refuge in the Embassy and it was arranged for Mrs. Maeztu to visit her husband in prison once a week on Tuesdays. Those who wanted to extricate him from jail were powerless against an increasingly divided rebel government then in the process of moving from Madrid to Valencia for safety and strategic reasons. The Argentinian delegation could not convince those in charge of the prison to let him go and neither were the arguments voiced by a former friend, Ricardo Baeza (ideologically separated from Maeztu), sufficient. He had incurred the ire of too many leftists and they considered him too valuable for release.

On October 1, 1936, in the city of Burgos, Francisco Franco Bahamonde was proclaimed Chief of the Spanish State. Meanwhile, José Antonio Primo de Rivera languished in a republican jail in Alicante, and Maeztu awaited his fate at the hands of revolutionaries. Permission for his wife's brief weekly visits was rescinded, and then his personal effects taken away; only by special allowance was he able to write a letter to his family. Sensing perhaps that his death was close, on October 28 he penciled two short notes to his wife that clearly reflect his concern for her and the son he would be leaving behind. That night, Maeztu recited to his prison companions Longfellow's "Hymn to Night." Shortly after midnight, on October

29 (third anniversary of the founding of the Falange), the name of a sixty-two year old right-winger was yelled out by the guards. Fifteen minutes later, after Maeztu had said goodbye to his friends, the sound of a pistol shot was heard in the entire prison.[27]

CHAPTER 3

The Revisionist Prose of the Early Years

A bibliographical rarity before reissuance in 1967, *Hacia otra España (Toward a New Spain)* is today a forgotten book, difficult to find even in the public libraries of Spain. Ramiro de Maeztu's first book exhibits a dogmatic and clipped style as befits a work of protest. It is a book of the times that not only reflects the historical moment and the social circumstances but also consitutes an indictment of the crises, movements, and concerns of that particular period. It is the most generational of Maeztu's works and quite possibly the only one that follows the line of the Generation of 1898. Maeztu had guessed the outcome of an uneven struggle from the incipient signs of rebellion, and bore no false hopes in view of overwhelming odds.

There is a pained concern for his country throughout the pages of *Hacia otra España (Toward a New Spain)* as little by little Maeztu details all that he finds negative in the Spain of old traditions, and cries out for a new nation, radically different from the traditional one. By calling for another Spain, Maeztu assumed that the possibility existed to make an old country new. The idea was, of course, absurd as he recognized years later when he told someone that ridding a nation of history was equal to dismissing from his own life the first fifty years of his existence. Even when writing this book, however, Maeztu confessed to not having the exact formula to rehabilitate his country materially and culturally. But his effort of analyzing the process and causes of the fall of Spain through the colonial wars, the disaster of 1898 at the hands of the United States, and subsequent socioeconomic crises at home is perceptive, and his avowed intent of regeneration, his basis for building a Spain for the future are enthusiastic and worthwhile.

I *The First Book*

Published in Bilbao and released in Madrid in February 1899, *Hacia otra España (Toward a New Spain)* appeared three months before Ramiro's twenty-fifth birthday. Biblioteca Vascongada was the publishing house (Fermín Herranz of this firm had also given Maeztu his first forum in a newspaper). In *El Porvenir Vasco*, Maeztu had written the first of the thousands of articles he would produce. *Toward a New Spain* has several antecedents, not the least of which are articles published in diverse newspapers and weekly magazines. Some thought pieces never reached print, while several essays were written expressly for this volume. There is a concerted effort to give the work some semblance of unity aside from the thematic, stylistic, and philosophic cohesion that Maeztu's writings enjoy. The pieces included date from August 1896 to September 1898 (presenting the reader with the before, during, and after of Spain's greatest political crisis up to the end of the nineteenth century). Accordingly, the author divides the book into three sections corresponding to the three periods mentioned: a) *Páginas sueltas (Loose Pages)*, b) *De las guerras (About War)*, and c) *Hacia otra España (Toward a New Spain)*. The last section, with the same title as the book itself, is fundamental, according to its author.

In each section, nevertheless, the foci remain constant: the role of the press during the crisis, intervention by the government and the Spaniards themselves, and the part played by the colonies overseas. Given its heterogeneity, the work will be approached from a thematic point of view taking the press, the government and internal affairs, and the colonies as bases for commentary. This triad is interrelated though not inextricably so. Maeztu and his generation felt that no issue was foreign to the problem or could not be tackled in his daily column.

Briefly, the book's mission (its author declared) was not to be the formulation of a master plan to get Spain back on her feet. He was right; at most *Toward a New Spain* offers partial solutions, some of which if implemented would doubtless have contributed to amelior-ate the deplorable situation the country was in—for example, the separation of commercial shipping from the navy command in "Las dos marinas" ("The Two Navies"). Other propositions either would not have changed conditions appreciably, or else they would have proved to be ineffectual and even counterproductive, as when he suggests cynically in "¡Aún es poco!" ("As If That Weren't Enough!")

that no one should go out of his way for love but rather that he should profit by it. Maeztu wants *Toward a New Spain* to serve the purpose of a documentary newsreel where the reader can review the impressions of a ruined nation and the interpretations of one intellectual as to the causes of the tragedy of 1898. Maeztu's pen is moved at all times by grief and indignation upon seeing Spain smaller than befitted her place in the world. He cites the falling of her navy from fourth to ninth place as a naval power in just over one year. Maeztu's desire is for his country to reawaken and grow. To this effect he feels he has a mission to fulfill with every one of his articles.

The most diverse part of the book is the first section, *Páginas sueltas (Loose Pages)*. Here no quarter is given any subject, especially Spain's eighteen million inhabitants (tolerant of a corrupt government and a self-indulgent press corps), oblivious to anything other than bullfighting or attendance at musicals and comedy reviews. The tone of bitter irony accentuates the author's loss of patience when he contemplates a general panorama of idleness, frivolity and self-deception. Spain was ripe for a disaster, yet only a few were cognizant of the real situation, and there was little they could do about it save for pointing out the danger signals. There is no clearly defined political ideology other than a stance against the status quo; Maeztu wants a change of policy, ideals, and behavior. His attitude is that of an alarmed realist who not only wants solutions that will work but demands them right away. His cry of alarm was drowned as he suspected it would be by the general agitation.

In his preface to the book's second part, *De las guerras (About War)*, Maeztu concedes that there are several contradictions to be found here, adding that nothing would have been easier than to unify his thought *a posteriori* before collecting these articles. Yet he states that he purposely left them unretouched in their second publication as examples of two major tendencies that have affected his thinking and the nation's: on the one hand, the historical, warlike, and heroic tendency, and on the other, the contemporary tendency, conservative yet positivistic. In those articles where Maeztu wisely seems to have anticipated the course of events—e.g., he advocated an early disengagement from the colonies—he appears to think himself deserving of merit. The educational years in Cuba receive the credit. With this remark the author returns once again to an attack against the foe within, of which he is a part—the press. Maeztu censures the press not for being ill-intentioned but for its indiscretion in reporting the war campaign. The press failed in its mission when it did not depict the ignorance of government leaders, the true and awesome power of the American fleet, and the real causes underlying the colonial uprisings. As usual when referring to the press, the pronoun Maeztu uses is "we." He realizes that at times the rigor and accuracy that characterize good reporting have not been his trademarks either, as when he views the United States as an imperial power bent on colonizing rather than granting independence to another nation's (Spain's) possessions. In this article, "Frente al conflicto" ("Facing the Conflict"), Maeztu's patriotic feelings get the best of him, and his emotions are caught up with those Spaniards going to war against the Yankee imperialists.

The key part of the book is the third and final set of five essays, the longest and best thought-out pieces of regenerationist prose of *Toward a New Spain*. Leaving behind all reference to the lost colonial empire, Maeztu concentrated on what remains for Spain to do. His hopes were pinned on an economic solution whereby the interior region of Castille would push itself up to the level of the prospering coastal areas. The methods advocated, however, are radical to the point of incompatibility with one another. Maeztu's praise of money as the answer to his country's social and political downturn falls nothing short of an embrace of the capitalist system, while, on the other hand, there is a socialistic undercurrent in Maeztu's advocacy of money as the incentive to get ahead in life as well as a means to rehabilitate the nation. Yet together, these two rival economic systems suited Spain's needs of that time. The first, capitalism, would be used initially to set the fiscal house in order and thus provide stability for a Marxist class struggle to take place subsequently. In other words, capitalism would be a necessary evil, a stage to be overcome in favor of a benign socialist state where there would be no privileged class and the worker in an age of industrialization would be justly rewarded for his labor.[1]

II　*The Campaign Against the Press*

Paradoxically, the target of Maeztu's harshest and most frequent criticism was the profession to which he himself belonged—the Madrid press corps. "Gente de letras" ("Men of Letters") is an inventory of the state of journalism. Here the author uncovers a damaging indictment that extends from simple newspapermen to respected authors of well-known works. The office of the journalist is the café, where he spends most of his waking hours. So the question of when a man entrusted to inform and guide the reading public does his own reading and thinking becomes an issue. Lack of serious dedication to one's profession is something Maeztu blamed on the 1898 war. He backs off a little, realizing that the press is not the only one to blame. Economic factors influenced the journalist directly, and the papers they worked for, but also touched those who, like Maeztu, felt the need to put together a book every few years. The blame for the generally low quality of newspapers (aside from the reporter's own carefree irresponsibility), falls on other intellectuals. Frequently an important author buttonholed a journalist, talking him into giving a buildup for a forthcoming book. Maeztu mentions this, noting that writers of stature were few at the time in Spain; an idea taken up again in the piece dedicated to Eusebio Blasco—a minor dramatist and short-story teller of the last half of the nineteenth century who enjoyed great success in his day, but is largely forgotten now. Although Maeztu's critical judgment fails him when he praises Blasco as a great author, his emphasis on this writer's work ethic (his efforts netted him a complete series that runs to twenty-seven volumes) is well taken. The exhortation pronounced by Maeztu at the end of this essay—"¡hay que trabajar mucho!" ("we have to work harder!")—is a constant thematic exhortation in *Toward a New Spain*. The hard-working author becomes a symbol for any hard-working man.

There are also others who feel the press's pernicious influence so directly that the results far overreach one individual's attitude or actions. Such a man is General Blanco, the protagonist of the piece *El General Leyenda* (*General Legend*), whose very title drips with irony. General Blanco (his real name), a soldier who had shown himself to be a prudent and wise military operator in the Philippines campaign, had been chastised incessantly in all the newspapers for not putting up a struggle in certain stages of the war when all resistance would have been senseless. Wounded in his pride as a man and as a soldier by the press's stinging charges, a few months later General Blanco intends to become General "Legend" as the commander of a 100,000 man garrison in Cuba. The catchy and very printable phrase "Victory or Death!" is the tragic phrase he wants history to remember him by, thus playing to the audience, represented by the press which now applauds him loudly for his melodramatic stance. In one of his most exaggerated attacks, Maeztu places the blame for the safety of the Spanish contingency in Cuba squarely on the shoulders of the news media, whose irresponsible attacks on the unblemished record of a general have impaired his judgment, placing in jeopardy the lives of 100,000 men.

That he was able to get away with such attacks can be explained only by his growing stature as a journalist as well as by the complete freedom from censorship that the press enjoyed in those days. But many members of the press corps remembered those emotionally charged denunciations when Maeztu became a conservative and nearly drove him from the profession, forcing him to write solely for a handful of right-wing publications. If Maeztu chastises the press so often and so intensely, it is because he overestimates its power. In three separate essays under the common title of "La Prensa" ("The Press"), the author again points an accusing finger. A failure to gauge public opinion properly is in Maeztu's view far from being the press' greatest fault during the war, since a newspaper's duty isn't just to reflect public opinion or even to just describe accurately a day's campaign. Some editors who tried to get by on news items and telegraph communiqués alone, from reporters in the field, soon found their circulation sales plummeting. The man in the street was quick to notice that a professional newsman's analysis was better informed than his own no matter how disingenuous the reporter. This demand, as Maeztu saw it, multiplied ten-fold the press' responsibility because a government by the press had virtually substituted the concept of popular sovereignity in all the Western European democratic countries. The crime lay not in having misjudged the nation, but in a dereliction of duty, especially the duty to inform fully.

Maeztu hammered accusations of a lack of meticulous, impartial, and worthy information that in other countries enlightened the citizenry about the state of the nation. In Spain, journalists were either incapable of making a correct appraisal out of sheer incompetence, or they sought to secure a favorable post through their influence as selectors of news items and manipulators of coverage of events. When the press cried for repression in the colonies, a move with which he might have concurred, Maeztu chided journalists for their lack of professionalism, insight, and common sense at seeing the waste and destruction while appeals to patriotism and victory in the name of history continued as headlines.

Picking up a Madrid newspaper one day, the author details in "Los diarios madrileños y la vida nacional" ("The Madrid Dailies and the National Scene") the contents of its news pages and the characteristic fourteen or fifteen columns. The topics were the most banal imaginable: bullfights, politicians' comings and goings, social news, theater reviews, and crimes; the latter is a topic which Maeztu takes up more than once. No notice was made of the national budget whose balance should have been every citizen's concern, no analysis of the industrial and agricultural backwardness, no mention of an education system badly in need of a thorough revision, indeed no notice can be found of the simmering regional separatist movements of the Basques and Catalonians until a local election was given limited coverage and the larger question figured as background material. The list of omissions offered by Maeztu seems interminable; he must have had difficulty restraining himself from enumerating all the lacunae of important newsworthy items. Maeztu overstates his case, charging the press with nothing less than the responsibility for informing, educating, and directing the affairs of all Spaniards. This is clearly an overestimation of the power of the news.

Although the Spanish press had forecast great national unrest if the overseas colonies were lost, neither the predicted military coup, civil war, or any other commotion ensued. Only a reawakening of separatist ideals seemed to linger in the aftermath of the thorough defeat. The miscalculations of the turn of events by newsmen was due, according to Maeztu, to the nearsightedness of the two-hundred and some odd journalists of Madrid and other large Spanish cities who read and wrote only with one another in mind, most of them with an eye to the more lucrative world of politics, or to praising a likely benefactor. This common practice contributed to the alienation of the reading public.

With almost no desire for outside sources of information, journalists found it increasingly difficult to explain the rekindling of separatist ideals. Their answer continued to be a stock one—Spain as a first rate national power was doomed. If this reply was as unimaginative as it was long lived, Maeztu's contention that it was the result of journalists' obfuscated interpretation of the news is an equally absurd reduction of the complex situation. Newsmen were remiss in their commitment to carry out worthwhile reporting and, true, they curried favor with the powerful, yet to say that they contributed directly to Spain's undoing is going too far. But Maeztu never closes the door completely: there is a chance for the press to return to the mainstream of the national consciousness. When it was realized that what the nation wanted was not better politics, but a total scrapping of the system, newspapers would be effective again. The press could resume its active role, welcoming radically new solutions to old problems and recommending their timely use, regaining its credibility while, more importantly, contributing to preservation of national unity and foiling the increasingly vocal separatists with a genuine campaign in the national interest. This could only come to pass if the political ambitions of every newsman were shelved. If nothing changed with newspapers, they would die as such, just like old style politics. This is wishful thinking by Maeztu, who expected the old ways to wither from lack of effectiveness, overlooking their entrenchment and the tendency of every institution for self-preservation.

The ingenuousness characteristic of Maeztu's sometimes visceral and candid reactions can be further observed in the article "La propaganda del crimen" ("Crime Advertising"). Here again blame for the spread of crime falls on the press. Maeztu considered that vivid description not only of the crime itself, but also of the ensuing judicial process (where an able defense attorney normally managed to prevent the deserved punishment), served two purposes, both noxious. First, the three to five columns taken up by criminal reports diminished the room available for "good news" reporting, or for "moral literature." Secondly, implying a duality of good and evil in man, Maeztu feared that the reader could not help be influenced into resolving his own life's conflicts by violence. Maeztu argues that man's moral fiber is pretty thin, and the animal within is all too easily roused by passion and irrational behavior.

The newspapers of the times have been found to have exerted negative influences on the Spanish people, misleading them with totally unrealistic estimates of the outcome of the war; on the government, for not challenging its policies or criticizing the corruption and incompetence among the leaders; on Spain's colonies overseas, for misjudging their worth which resulted in tremendous expenditures in terms of men and money; and, finally, the press' comportment seems to have had a bad influence on itself, leading to a loss of confidence by readers. Nothing in the way journalism behaved in this time of crisis appears praiseworthy to Maeztu. On the contrary, the crisis was in part due to a fundamental failure on the part of the press to act in a responsible manner. Only through self-cleansing and a totally different future course of action could newspapers regain their stature. The judgment was harsh, if accurate, but Maeztu felt that if any change was to be realized, it had to begin in the press itself.

III *The Blame on the Colonies*

At this stage Maeztu doubted that Spain's possessions in the New World were worth fighting for; consequently his views on Cuba, South America, and the Philippines, in general, are not very positive.

Certainly if judged by "El himno boliviano" ("The Bolivian National
Anthem"), the author's esteem for these countries is not high. Music
which he hears from an organ grinder while buying the morning
paper initiates a series of marked contrasts in Maeztu's mind. The
lyrics of the Bolivian National Anthem tell of a reality different from
what Maeztu himself remembered—the beatings and burnings to
which the inhabitants of Tegucigalpa were customarily subjected.
Ironically, while the melody praising Simón Bolívar and freedom
followed Maeztu down the street, he noticed an item in the
newspaper about two hundred people who received daily beatings
under orders from the Guatemalan president. This incident brought
to Maeztu's mind the anecdote of a certain Spanish envoy to Costa
Rica who complained to the president that one local daily frequently
directed insults to the Spanish colony. When the president asked the
representative what he wanted done with the newspaper, the
Spaniard answered that he only wished it would tone down its
language. So, when on the following day the police ransacked the
offices of the paper, the minister was astonished. His surprise was
even greater when the president declared that had the complainant
wanted the paper permanently silenced, he would have had the staff
hanged. Quoting Lacordaire's famous saying "Some people die
singing their immortality," Maeztu adds that, meanwhile, others will
languish into an uncounscious agony brought upon themselves. The
implication that Latin America, headed by tyrants, will go the first
route whereas Spain will die the second death is inescapable.

This loathing of tyrants and suppression becomes yet more
apparent in "El Czar en París" ("The Tsar's Visit to Paris"). Not even
France escaped Maeztu's notice given a conflict between the logical
and the practical. The event producing this contrast was the Tsar's
visit to the French capital. There, citizens of one of the more free
countries in Europe celebrated his appearance and welcomed him
enthusiastically. The French police force was allowed to search
buildings and private homes in order that no harm would befall the
Russian. Maeztu was amazed that a tyrannical ruler could be
accorded such a triumphant greeting. How, he asked, can an absolute
despot be acclaimed by a free people when his own subjects are mere
serfs? The only explanation resides in the inner character of Latin
man: a race of consuls and caesars. Never mind the French
Revolution or the Constitution of Cádiz; Latins deep down love the
worlds of Versailles and Aranjuez where absolute rulers did as they
pleased without regard for the millions of humans under them.

Consequently it shouldn't surprise anyone to behold the strong men who rule much of Latin America.

Maeztu's opposition to the Spanish colonies did not extend down to its peoples in a racist fashion as was the case with many Spaniards. The title of the article "La inferioridad del indio" ("The Inferiority of the Indians") is provocative and misleading, since the body of it is an intelligent and well-argued defense of the opposite view. Maeztu repeats the often-heard derogatory comments that the Indian sees his person as inferior to the white man, and thus he rebels against his own ethnic makeup; or that he has no ability for science due to his native apathy and lack of willpower, and consequently is kept from assimilating all the modern advances. As a result many claimed that it was a utopian dream to introduce progressive reforms in the Philippines. Maeztu rejected these notions, foreshadowing his future ideal of "Hispanidad" in favor of equality of man, and discrediting a racism that used intellectualism as a subterfuge. At that time (1896), when there were hardly more than twenty or so Philippinos in Madrid, a visit to the reading rooms of the Ateneo revealed that frequently these "Indians" outnumbered the Spaniards. It is wrong, argued Maeztu, to deny equal rights to a people who have adopted Spanish culture, language, and government, simply because of their facial features. They changed their way of life to accommodate the Spanish, from their religion to their language, but the one thing they could not change was their physical appearance. For that they should not be denied their rights. If reactionaries insisted upon their racist views, Maeztu warned, all they would achieve would be the loss of the Philippine Islands to the empire of the Rising Sun (Japan). Maeztu was proven right in his assumptions that Spain would lose this archipelago even if it did not cross his mind that it would come under the direct influence of the United States. The significance of these views lies in just how early Maeztu was attracted by the concept whereby all of Spain's offspring from the conquest would be welded together not by political ties but by bonds of language, tradition, religion, and culture. This would be his last dream, and apparently it was one that he nurtured for a long, long time.

Though critical of the colonies themselves in many respects, Maeztu also looked upon his own government as a culprit. He reflects on the huge number of Spanish recruits sent to Cuba. "27,000," the number of soldiers overseas, serves as the title of another essay. In it, Maeztu sarcastically laments that if these men had been the sons of cabinet officers, Spain would stand to lose future admirals, lawyers, and generals, but since those being sent to fight and die were only carpenters, masons, and farmers, why worry. In an allusion to the nineteenth-century British economist Thomas Malthus, Maeztu suggests scornfully that perhaps in the minds of the government leaders, Spain's eighteen million people represented overpopulation, and that a colonial war would bring it into check. The hyperbole is, of course, patent. Yet the indictment of the Spanish government is a ringing one.

That Maeztu truly did not want war can be deduced from a series of nine articles written in the first months of the year prior to the confrontation that he saw as inevitable. The chapter "Frente al conflicto" ("Facing the Conflict") collects the most significant fragments from the series. From the first to the last, we observe a growing awareness that armed confrontation was imminent. The government in Washington left the impression that it was gearing up its vessels for war, and although reason would lead Maeztu to believe that a country mindful of its democratic principles would not overrun another less powerful but equally sovereign state, all indications pointed to the determination of President McKinley to use force to solve the Cuban question. As for the Spanish newspapers that did not shy away from violence, Maeztu reminded them that violence itself was to blame for the situation at hand. Maeztu was not unfair in this criticism, nor did he take a position against the fighting men of Spain, but rather against his own government and the United States. As often as he had chastised the Madrid bureaucrats, the military, and the policy makers, there came a time when he felt he must close ranks with them. It happened when he learned that the U.S.S. *Maine's* captain, along with the ship's officers, was partying aboard another vessel instead of watching over his own ship, and Spaniards had to pull American sailors from the water but were nevertheless charged with maritime sabotage and calculated murder. Maeztu then felt that Spain had a duty to fight. He sided with his government knowing that the old wooden Spanish frigates were no match for the steel hulls of the United States' cruisers and destroyers with infinitely more effective firepower.

The weeks prior to the uneven encounter of both forces were a time of uncertainty for the Spanish side. In a last effort to avert war, Spain belatedly granted an armistice to the rebels. But it was a case of too little, too late. The Spanish government confronted a terrible dilemma: how to go to war although it now began to appear that a disastrous outcome was almost certain, and how to seek a more durable peace when its own people, egged on by the press, were feverishly asking for war. McKinley's message to Congress, whose text was reproduced in its entirety by the newspaper *El Imparcial*, made Maeztu wonder one more time if Cuba was worth the price. Unsuspectingly, neither Maeztu nor the vast majority of Spaniards felt that more than Cuba was at stake, when in fact Spain was gambling away all of its colonial remnants.

The option to fight was a painful one since the hope for victory was increasingly remote. Few really wanted war: the press, the vested interests that stood to profit from the manufacture and sale of war material, and both governments, especially Washington. Only certain political parties expected to gain something, and in Spain these did not have much support. In the U. S. Congress however, the right of the strong was solemnly proclaimed, a move that left the door open for a war where the expected booty was the spread of political influence bordering on territorial gain.

Maeztu had never been a strong advocate of democracy. Like his sometime friend, the philosopher Ortega y Gasset, he objected to rule by the will of the majority and favored instead rule by a select minority chosen on the basis of their ability to govern. Both, or Ortega at least, learned their lesson from Plato's *Republic* where a "democracy of the schools and not one of the polls"[2] is advocated. Maeztu, as the years went by, retreated further from this position and limited this elite minority to one—the dictatorship. His souring on democracy, even before the United States took up arms against Spain, can be seen in "El desarme" ("Disarmament"). Here the story is told of how the world's democracies increased their military arsenals while the supposed arch-enemy of the free nations, Tsarist Russia, sought and proclaimed peace in the world, advocating general disarmament. The paradox results, Maeztu asserted, solely because of a preconceived notion that one system is evil and the other is good. Instead we should draw our conclusions from the facts. If a democracy is not everything it purports to be, then maybe neither is an autocratic government all it is accused of being. What matters is not whether a democracy or an autocracy brings peace, but that it come.

Maeztu at this point had no faith in any form of government. So far he had criticized every type of rule, never showing the faintest praise for any. Government represented part of the status quo and this meant something to be torn down. According to Blanco Aguinaga, the essay "El sí a la muerte" ("A Yes to Death") seems to announce

Maeztu's future conservative ideology.[3] Indeed it does hint toward
that stage in life when he held tradition and a strong central power as
optimum political ideals. The article appeared after the battle of
Cavite where the Spaniards met defeat in the Philippines. Discour-
aged by this setback, Maeztu seriously considered putting a stop to
his writings, overwhelmed, as he put it, by the "eloquence of the
cannon and the telegraph."[4] But, he conceded that Spain had to say
yes to the war since her makeup had always been to fight. Herein lies
a contradiction. By accepting Spain's destiny as being based fundamentally on her past—she had always fought victoriously, and thus
was expected to follow the same course now—Maeztu negates his
former arguments. The contradiction, of which he warned his readers
in the preface to the book's second section, rises out of a slowly
awakening taste for war.

After the Cavite defeat, Maeztu awaited the results of upcoming
campaigns, expecting a victory if justice from those who "rule the fate
of all nations"[5] prevailed, but, in the event that Spain should fall, he
wanted her to go down in glory. If life could not be given the
affirmative, death should be welcomed without reservations. He
loathed those who in view of the gathering dark clouds prepared to
run away, saying that Spain's fall—should it come to that—ought to
be a noble gesture. Maeztu's hopes for a string of victories to reverse
Spain's first military failure did not materialize. So, embittered, he
could only look upon his country's former colonial subjects as traitors
to a nation who gave them the best she had to offer—too much of
herself.

The most hostile condemnation was directed toward the Cuban
business community in "La vara de medir" ("The Yardstick"). This
segment of the population, once ardent "defenders" of Spain's right
to rule the island, refused to pay the Spanish import tariffs following
the 1898 fiasco. Maeztu labelled them turncoats because of lack of
concern for Spain, opportunists willing to accommodate any government so long as a profit could be realized. When Spain ruled, the
businessmen were all for Spain, but now that the dominant power
was the United States, they were ready to forget their former master.
Moreover, Maeztu faulted the business class for fostering the
upheaval against Spain through an economic policy that strangled the
working classes as well as the wealthy landowner plagued by
mortgages and rising prices. Maeztu suggested that the political
conflict was not really the most important. It was the unrest brought
about by the greedy fiscal policies of the business class that drove
Cubans to seek a scapegoat in their ruler—Spain.

In the end Maeztu felt that it was best to forget what could no longer be helped. This theme inspires the final essay of the section *De las guerras* (*About War*). Entitled "Dolor que pasa" ("The Pain Goes Away"), this piece offers a marked contrast between the impressions aroused by the arrival in Bilbao of a shipload of returning combatants from Cuba and the disinterested attitude of those who witnessed the homecoming. The men, their bodies wasted by starvation, fever, and the punishment of war, told of their misfortunes; but their story had already been told many times over. Only their disfigured features spoke eloquently enough about the ordeal undergone. Nonetheless Maeztu ends this section of *Toward a New Spain* on a positive note. The following morning sunshine and music envigorate Bilbao. Zest for living inundates the city suggesting a fresh start, literally a new dawn symbolizing Spain's brighter future.

IV   *The Government and the People*

In a work so preoccupied with a nation's welfare one would expect to find the greater part dedicated to government and internal affairs. And such is the case with this author's first book. Out of the total of thirty-seven essays, nearly two-thirds are concerned with the two topics mentioned and, significantly, the very first essay of the book falls into this category.

The final decades of the nineteenth century, called the Restoration Period (lasting until 1905), were labelled by Ortega as the "silly years" due to the tenor which characterized the times, e.g., the bullfights, cheap journalism, melodramatic theater, and a general lack of civil concern.[6] Maeztu seized upon a catchy phrase, "progressive paralysis," that the newspaper *El Liberal* used to describe Spain's ills. Concurring eagerly, he expanded on the idea demonstrating the correctness of the diagnosis. Citing as evidence the dissolution of all major political parties in the last twenty years, Maeztu pointed to the power plays by political bosses, as well as the lack of interest by Spaniards in the body politic as shown by the poor readership of political columns in the daily newspapers. He further examined the ailment, subdividing it into the intellectual, the moral, and the imaginative paralyses. The first he saw reflected in the bookstores crowded with unsalable volumes, in the university posts occupied by incompetent professors, in the newspapers empty of ideas, in the near-empty National Library, and in the theaters where only artless playlets found favor with audiences. In the second category he quoted the incredible prices that people were willing to pay to witness a bullfight or purchase an expensive package of cigarettes. And in the third instance, Maeztu decried the abandonment of the ideals and enthusiasm of the Spanish race.

Part of this "paralysis" could have been overcome, as we see in the article "Símbolos" ("Symbols") where Maeztu applauded the interest shown by Madrid's citizens in a play whose characters the author considered symbols of the true state of Spanish life. One by one he explained the significance of each character. There was the typical man without talents who by influence moved from the newsroom to a governor's mansion in the provinces. The man's widow who, after his death, could not do without all the luxuries to which she had grown accustomed in Madrid's artificial lifestyle willingly traded her future for a yard of fine cloth. The wheeler-dealer, so eager to make a profit that he ignored every law in the code, in the end fell prey to his own insatiable appetites. Finally, the children of the deceased, portrayed as defenseless victims, symbolized the orphaned Spain wondering what destiny held for her when the colonial disasters became a thing of the past. Ironically, for this sickness the cure should be Spain's youth.

V   *The Role of Youth*

Taking another angle, this time focusing on youth as independent from their adult guardians, Maeztu pointed to the carefree university graduates without ideas or ideals. At this point the author took his famous stand that perhaps it would be better to leave Spain alone in her wheelchair and let her die without reproach. Youth, it appears, could not yet redeem the country since the system had affected them as well. In the book's opening essay, "Nuestra educación" ("Our Educational System"), Maeztu cynically railed against an antiquated education that did not equip an individual to wage a successful economic battle in life. Reviewing the fortunes of former classmates and friends, he recounts in detail the bad luck of the good student for whom excellence in education has proven useless. Only three of his acquaintances have achieved success. One married a wealthy woman; one made his fortune by quitting school and starting up a liquor distillery business in Cuba. The last went to England to learn how to make shoes, setting up a manufacturing establishment upon his return to Spain. The author himself denies being able to live comfortably off his pen. Maeztu's greatest concern in this particular essay are the years lost by Spain's university graduates, largely unequipped to fend for themselves in the world.

The inversion of social values brought about by a predominance of the worst people in the ruling positions of government drove Maeztu to look for new leaders with a will to eradicate the misguided policies that carried the nation to its ruin. The 1898 defeat could have proven to be beneficial in the long run had it served to rid the country of corrupt and idle leaders, proven wrong time and again by the extent of the losses in the war. Spain needed enlightened individuals to replace the old guard and bring about reform. This group could only be constituted by her youth, as ill-prepared as many considered them to be.

The last essay of the book, "Contra la noción de la justicia" ("Against the Concept of Justice"), is divided into two briefer pieces of which the first, entitled "Como trabajan los pensadores nuevos" ("How the New Thinkers Work"), amounts to a fervent defense of the young generation of intellectuals. Oddly enough, Maeztu does not consider himself one of its members, even though he was then twenty-four years old. He admired this new generation for the way its members went quietly about their work, many choosing to travel to learn better methods and techniques with which to improve old ways. As a result, upon their return, new factories cropped up, agricultural yields increased and the fruits of efficiency could be seen. Maeztu, along with the rest of the Generation of 1898, belonged unquestionably to the theoretical rather than pragmatic thinkers, since none of them made an impact except in the intellectual and literary spheres. But the practical aspect concerned Maeztu much more at this time.

When the youths he praised were accused of a lack of exuberance and an apparent cold-bloodedness, Maeztu defended them. This new breed of intellectuals did not care about many things that excited the rest of the nation, such as social justice or humanity's progress. They were not immoral because of it however, but rather amoral; their energies and attention were channeled into their work, which many considered a mission. They were interested almost exclusively in intellectual pursuits capable of yielding sure material results. And the times favored them since Spain's history, now that her empire and army lay in ruins, no longer concerned many. Her glorious past, which might have hindered the kind of program Maeztu wanted, no longer mattered. In this youth Maeztu saw a chance to produce a new Spain of an importance equal to that enjoyed in the Golden Age. But the number of talented and dedicated individuals able to gain a foothold in the positions of power was so small that the results Maeztu had hoped for were greatly overestimated. The idealism of Spain's youth was not translated into any meaningful action; for the most part they turned out to be the equals of their elders.

VI *The Models for the Future*

The book's fourth essay, "Las quejas de Raventós" ("Mr. Raventós' Complaints"), presents Maeztu's ideal Spaniard. The farmer Raventós protests that, after travelling to Madrid and cutting through all the bureaucratic red tape to lower the farmers' taxes some twenty percent, no one who benefitted through his efforts offered either a word of gratitude or helped with expenses. Raventós claims that by this indifference his colleagues demonstrate an amazing lack of knowledge in the running of their businesses since farming constitutes not only working the land but also looking out for the common interest of all farmers. Maeztu capitalized upon this curious incident to point to the scarcity of men like Raventós, especially in high places. In his usual manner, Maeztu classified men into two main groups: those who know their profession, and those who ignore the full import of theirs. Unfortunately, Maeztu writes, for some strange reason the ranks of the social values had been inverted and the second group prevailed for decades in the ruling of Spain. Maeztu speaks as the apologist for a new man who, like Raventós, will lay aside the Spaniard's typical bad habits—really a superman in the Nieztschean sense.

If Raventós becomes the ideal man, Bilbao symbolizes the model city. A look at this Basque capital serves to give Maeztu a forum on behalf of industrial growth, the riches it presupposes and the ultimate meaning it will very likely have. Much like Barcelona earlier, Bilbao had reached an important level of industrial strength. Yet Maeztu was not a proponent of wealth for its own sake; instead he pointed to the beautiful chalets, the clean streets, the appetite for the fine things in life on the part of the new rich, such as fine paintings even if they were purchased for their exaggerated frames, for private libraries even if leather bindings and gold edges were a primary factor in the selection. Maeztu felt that only when people reached this level of prosperity would art also prosper. What did it matter if Bilbao's citizens bought season tickets to their opera or the theater, and then did not bother to appear at the performance? The orchestra as well as the actors would survive, and that was more important. Slowly the public would be drawn in until one day it became caught up in the realm of art. Power and money thus would ultimately be turned into something beneficial.

If one believes in the principles of capitalism, Maeztu is right. A realist, he knows from experience that neither altruism nor patriotism make men ambitious or efficient, but money and the profit motive do. So that when he praises gold in "Contra la noción de la justicia" ("Against the Concept of Justice") or when he advances the theory of a "reverence for money," in a maligned essay by the same title, Maeztu is simply advocating capitalism. The profit incentive and not Joaquín Costa's *política hidráulica* would change the face of Spain, since not only would men strive to excel, but the smartest would come out on top, thus negating the specter of nepotism, influence peddling, and inefficiency that had led to Spain's economic, social, and political downturn. Regeneration was possible but only if extraordinary steps were taken.

VII   *Spain's Negative and Positive Aspects*

Toward a New Spain represents Maeztu's earliest thought, by no means organized as a system yet recognizable for its strong opinions and clear-cut ideas. Maeztu found plenty wrong with Spain. She had lost her link with Europe—the modern world and the currents of progress. She had forgotten how to produce great men. Maeztu scorns the universities with their meaningless diplomas that turned out young people without consciousness of duty, unable to pay their own way. This particularly enraged Maeztu who was an impassioned worker throughout his life while others around him either led a dissipated life in the cafés and streets of Madrid or were unable to find work to suit their qualifications.

Another of Maeztu's negative findings was that Spain allowed herself to be governed by the worst individuals. The leadership for many years had been made up of idle men, men of deceit and empty promises instead of men of action, work, and high ideals. Maeztu believed that Spain had embarked on enterprises superior to her means even when her best men realized that such campaigns were undermining her strength. The discovery and colonization of America, and fighting the Counterreformation debilitated her beyond recovery. Now in 1898, exhausted, she was suffering the consequences of her quixotic undertakings. In opposition to the colonial enterprise, Maeztu called for an end to such efforts, attacking the politicians for engaging in wars without familiarizing themselves with the issues and without taking stock of the enemy. Newspapers shared the blame for their prowar campaigns, their misinformed reporting, and bellicose editorials. Maeztu saw that Spain had not overcome her internal division or old habits, creating new ideals and renovating herself. When the war hawks and the doves argued, it represented the two Spains confronting each other in the form of the "traditional instinct" on the one hand and the "critical instinct" on the other. Maeztu viewed Spain as a bankrupt country, save for the northern and northeastern coastal areas which had identified themselves with the industrial movement of a more modern world outside Spain's borders. It is not wonder then that the author cried out for a new Spain.

His revisionist attitude led him to propose a number of solutions. Among the most important is his advice that Spain should try to raise its standard of living to the European level by encouraging further the incipient coastal industrial development in the hope that it would spread to the interior. This could have been done by the moneyed middle class then beginning to control and develop coal, textiles, and banks. Castille was to renew its agricultural preponderance, modernizing its cultivation processes via the introduction of chemical fertilizers, more efficient irrigation, and by creating schools of agriculture, or by sending the future farmers abroad to learn. Spain must engage as well in a true cultural expansion, producing a new youth willing to work ably, whose ideals should coincide with the best interests of their country; an intelligent youth disinterested in conspiracies, apolitical, eager to cooperate in the generating of a new social state by applying their newly acquired scientific knowledge. Maeztu wanted a youth with a new and healthy attitude, possessed of the strength to fight against old ideas and traditions. For him a new generation, which turned out to be the famous Generation of 1898, could raise Spain from her ruins.

VIII *The Repudiation of the Book*

Toward a New Spain, then, underscores the need for material progress[7] derived from an intellectual element—youth—and a need to look to the future instead of banking hopes on a glorious but irretrievable past. Maeztu's call for a new order included proposals he later regretted, especially his demand that Spain disassociate herself from the colonies abroad. His most cited work, *Defensa de la Hispanidad (In Defense of Hispanism),* represents a complete reversal of this attitude. In it, the former colonies and the founding country are seen as inextricably united by a common cultural bond that decides the course of their future. This was perhaps the main reason for the author's repudiation of this, his first book, though also paramount was the mistake he himself recognized years later of advocating that Spain become another country, without realizing that by eschewing her past Spain would stop being herself. His judgment about *Toward a New Spain* may have been as harsh as the book itself was. He said: "All of its pages deserve to be burned, but the title expresses the ideal of 1898 and of the present day."[8]

CHAPTER 4

Back to the Middle Ages

IN London in 1916 Maeztu published a work titled *Authority, Liberty and Function in the Light of the War*. Written in English, it reappeared in a Spanish version under the title *La crisis del humanismo (The Crisis of Humanism)* three years later. The two are essentially the same book save for the examples offered peculiar to each nation or to the references made concerning an ongoing World War I in the first instance and a resolved conflict in the second. The contents, relatively long essays by the author's standards, had appeared earlier, between March 1915 and June of the following year, in the English journal *The New Age* and in popular Spanish periodicals.

The flaws are all very familiar: lack of unity, repetitiveness, instant judgments nullified by passing time, and references to circumstances obscure in the long run. In spite of these shortcomings, Maeztu felt strongly enough about *Authority* . . . to reissue it in Spain in 1919. His awareness of part of the objections noted shows in the more polished and less rambling Spanish version. But even without these largely superficial alterations, two virtues rescue the work from the run-of-the-mill annual collection of a journalist's best efforts masquerading as a book. It possesses an organic cohesiveness which leads one to believe that its pages were written having in mind their place in the larger context of a fully conceived work. Secondly, this collected effort represents a turning point in Maeztu's thought, from the rebellious liberalism evidenced in *Toward a New Spain* to a more conservative and paternalistic socialism. This change of orientation can be attributed to his firsthand experiences in the great conflict, shared with his friend T. E. Hulme, and his growing inclination toward socialism and the virtues of the collective work of people.

The change actually began as far back as 1911, when Maeztu left for the University of Marburg, a center of philosophic Rationalism. There he learned German and wrestled with the philosophy of Kant and his idealist aprioristic concepts. Others whom he read and probably understood better included Nicolai Hartman (phenomenological thought), Jacques Maritain (Thomism), and his personal friend Hulme (original sin). All of them drove from his head the ideas acquired from Croce's *Philosophy of the Spirit*, which had first pulled him away from the Church. Initially there came a religious redirection or "conversion" as some—over Maeztu's protests—called it, followed by a sociopolitical change. In this perspective, it is not difficult to understand Maeztu's response to the First World War, his weighing of its legacy, and the hopeful recommendations advanced for the future avoidance of a similar holocaust. In these pages, the critique of modern history belies a very real awareness of recent personal appraisal and redirection. The English title *Authority, Liberty and Function* . . . refers to the three parts of the book, "Authority and Power" "Liberty and Happiness," "Function and Values," seen by Maeztu as three unique variations of social organization through the modern age. The Spanish title, *La crisis del humanismo (The Crisis of Humanism)*, alludes to the great theme of that work, Maeztu's overriding concern with the mistaken direction in which mankind had been moving ever since the Renaissance years.

I *Authority*

The basis for Maeztu's belief that he can offer a worthwhile treatise which would organize society and its government under a new structure is fundamentally religious. The Renaissance's ultimate effect was to make man forget his ephemeral nature and his subservience to a superior being, principles that had guided him for over twelve centuries. Humanism's secular exaltation brought about the change from a theocentric to an anthropocentric society that led to governments whose laws totally disregarded limiting principles. From this, a cycle of self-engendering crises resulted, culminating in the greatest of all conflicts, the World War. Maeztu asks that man turn back to the fifteenth-century crossroads and instead of following in the direction of secular humanism, take the road marked religious humanism away from egotism, chaos, and annihilation and toward the recognition of his finite, sinful and God-fearing nature. The humble recognition of original sin is viewed by Maeztu as the only possible first step toward a more sane world order. This is indeed quite a switch from the ultraliberal who ignored any traditional belief, religious or otherwise, unless to denigrate it. This change was due in large part to his brief but close personal friendship with T. E. Hulme, as Maeztu himself admits. This indebtedness cannot be overstressed. Maeztu understood men better than their books, and felt deep admiration and kinship for the British thinker. Hulme's body of writings is truly so small that his life and actions spoke as eloquently about his philosophy of the fallen condition of man as his publications could have.

Maeztu quarrels with the viewpoint which attributes solely to the Middle Ages the belief that man is a sinner and his world a vale of tears. For the author both assumptions signal a cognizance of the human condition characteristic of all historical periods. The new centers of learning established in Toledo, Córdoba, and Palermo further dispelled theocentric notions in every order of human endeavor, social, political, religious, economic, artistic, or intellectual. With the Renaissance, man and not God became the center of all things. The humanists secularized the Church and deified their own image. As creators of art, the immortals of this period produced masterpieces so perfect that the greatness grew with time, but the consequence of such achievements, Maeztu contends, was the transferral of perfection from the art to its creator. The reasoning went that if the work was good or perfect it followed that the artist must be also inherently so. Patently false though this non sequitur is, Renaissance man was convinced of his position at the center of the universe. Through his false humanist ethics man lost all fear of God and became a law unto himself. Subjectivism to this degree led only to infringement on the rights of others and ultimately brought the necessity for a check on man's freedom.

Out of this practical necessity for social order, first noted by Hobbes, grew the centralized power of the modern State. As the British political philosopher saw it, however, the State had no moral mission, only an authoritarian one—to see that contracts were fulfilled. Rousseau who, contrary to Hobbes, believed in man's innate goodness, advocated a State that would protect the individual's rights. Though their philosophies differ, the results are the same— the State assumes supreme power. Hobbes demanded unconditional submission to an absolute ruler without safeguards against his possible shortcomings. Rousseau asked that the rule, not of one man, but of an undefined "general will" be accepted unquestioningly. One opens the way for tyrannical rule, the other fails to explain general will or prove its existence.

The modern tendency to conceive the State as a single ruling concentration of power was counterbalanced in the Middle Ages by a distribution of authority. For Maeztu, then, there existed a much wider choice than authoritarianism or anarchy as Hobbes threatened. The alternative was a balance of power, not only within a nation but among the family of nations as well. The guild system is what he had in mind, a structure that crumbled before the Renaissance's trumpeted worth of the individual. In medieval times, a man's rights were based on his guild membership as a carpenter or brickmason. Then came the humanists and convinced him that his duty was no longer to his trade but to himself. Soon thereafter the guild system began to disintegrate, and the power vacuum resulting from its disappearance was filled progressively by the strong centralized State.

The belief that a unification of power was indispensable to provide a social order began to wane in the nineteenth century. When the State tried to eradicate completely the few remaining guilds, the workers themselves sought to establish new labor unions. As a progression from their origin in the medieval guilds the members of these unions enjoyed not only their professional privileges but also their rights as citizens. Power was now shared equally, at least in theory, among workers and their government. England became the prime example and Maeztu learned quickly the advantages of guild socialism, though he never guessed the ultimate harm of the labor movement's growing ability to wreak havoc with the economics of a nation and subsequently its political machinery and social welfare— again England would be a good example.

Germany was another matter. Maeztu viewed it as a country that until 1914 firmly believed in the concept of a unified power State as more than a necessity. He reasoned that had they considered it only as a necessary evil (Hobbes), the Germans would have ceased upholding it as such when conditions no longer dictated its usefulness. The only conclusion was that Germany no longer considered the State as a necessary evil but as something intrinsically good, to be preserved even when no longer needed. The State had become "not only a political invention, but an ethical idea" (27).[1] The corollaries are not hard to guess. For example, when the State carries out an action on its own behalf, the said acts are automatically good ones. This fallacious reasoning has its clear ascendancy in the Renaissance belief that a masterpiece proves the perfection of its creator. Maeztu's intention was to show the error undermining the notion that the State can exist as a good through rapid examination of Kant and the German idealists' political thought.

Kant preached unconditional obedience to Authority. His logic is not founded on the inherent goodness of an act performed by the State but rather on the expediency of such an act. A centralized State was as imperative in Kant's mind as it had been in Hobbes' and Rousseau's. Fichte's writings and speeches reveal much the same advocacy for an all-powerful central government. Hegel, his successor, the culminating figure of German Idealism, was in all likelihood the first to conceive an ontological panorama of the State seen as a product of reason and the ideal place for the development of morality.[2] His widely known argument that the State enjoy undisputed authority through "organized freedom" endeared him to the Prussian government which, in turn, can be considered as the Hegelian State par excellence.[3]

Maeztu, who disagreed with all of Hegel's predecessors, is even more opposed to him. He shares the philosopher's opinion that ideally the State, rather than being an entity, constitutes only a relationship between the governor and the governed—a judicial or legal relationship since it is basically a fulfillment of contracts. For Maeztu these relations are just when the State is good, evil when it is not. Here the two part company because the State, in Hegel's thinking, is identified with Good and needs only to act in order to be right. Its only duty is to ensure its autonomy and enlarge its power. The governed, meanwhile, are morally bound to obey the State since the supreme authority of the governor implies the absolute obedience of the governed. Such a State could only prosper so long as its borders expanded. In this manner its citizens would remain hopeful that in spite of their subservience they themselves might become governors (i.e., oppressors) through their nation's dominance of foreign territory. The flaw of such a political regime lies in its insatiable appetite at the expense of a limited number of adversaries, one of which would be bound to be more powerful in time.

The idealist and humanist theories surveyed left Maeztu convinced that the principles of Christian morality are founded on a more solid footing than any of the formal ethics discussed. He saw man as a means to goodness, so created explicitly by God, not as an end unto himself. No general will exists for him; only individuals have a will of their own. However, something may be desired commonly by a plurality of individuals. When what is sought is good, then the association becomes good and its purpose legitimate. In turn, its approach to the circumstances of the given situation is the origin of true authority. This should be considered the sole source of legitimate authority. It is an objective morality completely opposite to the German subjectivism founded originally on the equivocal principles of secular humanism.

II *Power*

Aware of the perils entailed in the accumulation of power for its own sake, Maeztu points out that the single-minded pursuit of Truth, Justice, and Love can turn out to be equally undesirable. Yet the unity of these four ideals, which he identifies with God, lies by dint of its magnitude beyond man's reach. Since singly possessed they represent an individual and social danger, and unified they are unattainable, man's reach for any one of them must keep the remainder in sight.

Maeztu divides power into two main classifications: personal and social. These are further subdivided into another two categories. In all, an unequal distribution of power is found among men, a corollary of Maeztu's undeclared belief that men are not created equal—an opinion shared by Ortega y Gasset who considered that the twentieth century's gravest error lay in holding all men as equals.[4] Ortega opposed the notion of superiority as forcefully, however—for him men not being equal meant just that, that men were different, not necessarily that some were better than others. In espousing this view Maeztu thought that there were variable quantities of power or energy in men. By personal power he meant talent, health, will power, all of which could be spent in the form of "free energy" as man wished such as for play and diversion or as "chained energy" intended for a constructive and definite purpose like work. But social power was the most important. Wealth, education, and social position are its manifestations.

Once again "free" and "functional" are the two kinds of energy found under the second classification. The curtailment of the majority's personal power accruing to each integrating individual, for the sake of a single person about to take charge, gives rise to social power. Social power must be linked to a specific function, given only with limits and for predetermined reasons so that it can be exercised solely on behalf of decided values or enterprises. Only in this fashion can tyranny be avoided.

The question of how to stop that social injustice derived from the abuse of power—tyranny—remains in Maeztu's view the leading motive for debate over the hegemony between military and economic power. Maeztu points to Marx and Dühring as the leading authorities behind the two points of view. In Marxist terms, economic power is intrinsically superior to military and even political power. Dühring, on the other hand, felt that military relationships are the basis of history, whereas economic considerations are merely ancillary. Marx's constituted a materialist philosophy, Dühring's an idealist one. Marx contradicted himself, and his followers are worse sinners in this respect; military muscle has proven itself more useful repeatedly, for Marxists of all colors, than economic might. Dühring's *Gewalttheorie* has been just as wanting, e.g. the case of armies crippled by scarcity of supplies for lack of economic resources— money equips, funds, and maintains a military force of whatever size.

Maeztu felt no logical compulsion to choose between military or economic power. Instead, he took a larger view which enabled him to accommodate opposites. Maeztu views both as different manifestations of a same source: power. Though "Power," he wrote, "is one, its forms are many" (61). Consequently, for him an industrial and a military state are not incompatible. Pointing out how England and the United States, in the course of a few years, rose to military supremacy from economic beginnings is Maeztu's way of debunking the notion that one must dominate and exclude the other.

In the final discussion of what constitutes the nature of the modern authoritarian state for Maeztu and the implicit leading causes of World War I, he examines two tendencies prevalent in the relationship between power and law, or might and right. Might, Maeztu feels, is a condition of all historical realities. Right, on the other hand, is only a property of some realities (63). The choice apparent is either a correlation of the two, or an independence where neither concept includes the other. At the time the prevailing theory was to identify power and law—the pacifists by saying that right was might, and the militarists by taking the opposite tack. The pacifist must believe that law includes power and that the latter is not independent of the former. In reality nevertheless, Maeztu affirms, pacifists are not consistent with this notion and instead consider right to be quite separate from might declaring that the first should override the second—a contradiction since they are considered independent and thus incapable of affecting one another. Whether a pacifist obeys, ignores, or resists the authority of a military government, he will only succeed in proving that law and power have nothing in common.

This line of thought, dominant in England prior to World War I, did not originate there but in Kantian Germany a century earlier. There, might submitted to right until 1848 when the practical results were the defeat of German Idealism (70). It was then that Germany stopped believing that law in itself was power and became convinced of the contrary—anything that triumphed was just (70–71). The militarist argues that power in and of itself is justice. Both the masses and the intellectual minority maintained this view in prewar Germany. Ostwald preached that the will of the law could not be separate from that of the individual—an idea sowed earlier by Kant that Maeztu rejected. The mass mentality took this to mean that there was no law but that represented by power. On the intellectual level, the similar ideas of Sellinek, a professor at the University of Heidelberg, spread and became the government line—for him also the State and power were one. In the end both pacifist (British) and militarist (German) views converge as a result of their inadequacies—power either becomes the pillar of law or else the latter becomes a theoretical accessory to the former.

If neither a militaristic nor a pacifist stance satisfies Maeztu's criterion for an equitable and viable state, neither does the manifestation of power through economic dogmatism. He eschewed economics as a discipline because of its generalizing tendencies, as well as for a genuine personal dislike for Karl Marx whom he viewed as the "agitator" responsible for the chaotic economic interpretation of history. Maeztu recalls that only when usury—"a sin in theory and a crime in practice" (121)—became a condoned business practice, did economics attain such import. The next logical misstep occurred in the seventeenth century when the British economist Nicholas Barbon ensured the triumph of capitalism by introducing the then revolutionary notion that an object's value was not intrinsic but what the market or the buyer placed on it. This Maeztu rejected on two counts: first, because it meant a total subjectivization of value; secondly, because capitalism means that a minority normally controls wealth and industries, creating a working class which is unable to avoid looking at life in strictly economic terms (120). Marxism dehumanizes history, capitalism dehumanizes man, Maeztu seems to be saying—neither fulfills the promises of humanism. Adam Smith's liberal idea that out of man's free exchange would come only good things was for Maeztu an ingenuous hope. Economic liberation could signal only a competition for wealth. And the larger the stakes, the greater the danger, as the World War had shown. Such apocalyptic visions were not far off, as the Second World War demonstrated, yet the reasoning behind them obviously was, as were the reasons for the hope that a new dawn might be coming. The estimation that man, at that moment, was once again on the verge of becoming a bearer of cultural values (39) akin to his medieval ancestor, and therefore more obedient to his Creator strikes today's reader as far off the mark. Such an illusion smacks of religious fervor, not of an historical or even sociological rationale. Moral ends, Maeztu forgot, do not frequently rule economic policies.

In the course of *The Crisis of Humanism*, Maeztu has been seeking the remote as well as the more immediate causes of the First World War. The last essay of the first part focuses on the role played by bureaucracies in the outbreak of the conflict, one of the seemingly less important contributing factors. Maeztu understood bureaucrats to be all those persons whose salaries are paid by the State and whose allegiance, therefore, belonged to the State, a nationalist class whose ideal and provider are the same. Another characterizing trait of bureaucracies is their tendency toward the enlargement of their own ranks. No competition exists in the bureaucracy that would dictate salaries—these are fixed—and moreover, the greater the number of bureaucrats in a given agency, the greater the importance such a branch acquires, and therefore the greater the opportunity to advance in rank. Only when the fiscal demands reach proportions too burdensome to bear will nonbureaucrats no longer consider it worthwhile to work on behalf of the State—some will emigrate but others will choose a more active role and fight against the State. Before reaching such an intolerable stage, the bureaucracy looks to the outside for expansion. England did it and the British empire was born; Holland, Portugal, and Spain also met with considerable success in their colonial efforts. The solution Maeztu offers to the spread of bureaucracies and the ultimate consequence of their proliferation is the organization of producing (i.e., nonbureaucratic) classes into societies to control state expenditures. This would be done by means of professional organizations, much in the same manner that medieval guilds checked the spending of kings and feudal lords. Maeztu thus is looking to the past for solutions to the future, or rather giving an oversimplified answer to an immensely complicated dilemma. To state unequivocally that the sole means of tackling the problem of self-enlarging bureaucracies (whose appetite for growth fostered a World War) is to look back to the past, much as Renaissance man prepared for the future by emulating the ancient Greeks, and is a distortion in perspective.

Maeztu attempted to demonstrate the failure of authority as a basis for constituting a national society. "Man emancipated himself from his ultra-human gods for which he had lived in better times, proclaimed himself the spiritual center of life and ended up by finding that center in a single man or a small group of men whom he deified labelling them the State" (111). If in the name of order a central authority is instituted, this authority will be useful, but only insofar as it fulfills one primary function—to maintain order with the moral consent of the ruled. When order is based solely on authority instead of the opposite, loss of civil and social rights results.

For Maeztu, when authority is the basis for a society, one of two things happens: 1) the State opposes all other values (science, art, philosophy, etc.), sealing its own destruction, or 2) the State does not discourage humanist pursuits and thus becomes one of enlightened despotism. Since absolute power always leans toward increasing its scope, a fact known to more liberally constituted societies, a coalition eventually forms to oppose expansion. The menace of a universal conflict is a consequence of society's establishment on the basis of authority, whether it be economic, military, bureaucratic, despotic, or a "general will." The evil nature of man leads him inevitably to "maximum disorder" upon his assumption of a position of authority.

III *Liberty*

Once the hope had been voiced that nations decentralize the authoritarian power of the State in order to avoid repetition of the war just past, then Maeztu asked whether other obstacles existed to the distribution of power. The answer, of course, is affirmative. For Maeztu the ideal of liberty constituted such a hindrance. He saw in post nineteenth-century liberalism a total devotion to the individual's privileges. Whereas freedom of individuals once meant the roots of a democratic regime, the same no longer held true. Maeztu considered a democracy to mean government of the people for the people. Liberalism connoted for him the idea of the individual respected as an absolute value; in other words, government for the benefit of the majority versus government for the individual, which amounts to none, since complete independence defies social discipline. Not that Maeztu considered liberty incompatible with democracy. He felt that, paradoxically, there was such a thing as organized, structured, lawful freedom.

Democracy has as its basis the pursuit of a common goal by a given number of individuals constituted in a social order. The organization

alluded to here by Maeztu is national defense—"To organize is
simply to unite men under certain rules for the attainment of a
common end by means of the division of their labor" (143)—although
it could have been any other national goal. Democracy would appear
capable of redistributing the overconcentration of power held by the
State so disastrously up to World War I, if it weren't for the
individual's self-aggrandizement under liberalism, born out of the
Renaissance's equivocal humanistic deviations.

Several other objections to liberty as a governing principle exist,
which Maeztu debunks to his own satisfaction. The first one focuses
on the misconception of relative leniency of democracy's laws
compared to the laws that rule an autocratic State. The elected leader,
contends Maeztu, enjoys more power than the autocrat since it was
conferred upon him by people who will add their efforts to his. The
error here is that the electors will only work insofar as the chosen
ruler works to reach a popularly set goal. A second defense of
controlled liberty, i.e. democracy as Maeztu understood it, turns out
to be slightly less unconvincing. It deals with the masses' ability to
govern themselves, a problem which Ortega y Gasset faced squarely
in his *La rebelión de las masas (The Rebellion of the Masses).*[5] The
issue lies in the overall incompetence of the average man to make
major decisions affecting his own and his fellow citizens' destinies,
says Ortega, and Maeztu agrees in part. Yet incompetence is not
endemic to democracies, it is found in monarchies and aristocracies as
often, Maeztu goes on to say. Furthermore the larger the number
who become able governors, the greater the good of the democracy as
it approaches total participation.

Liberalism becomes the greatest danger to democracy when it
glorifies the individual to the detriment of his fellow citizens. Maeztu
decries the emphasis placed by John Stuart Mill on the independence
of the individual. On a practical level, democracy can only thrive on
limited, if equal, freedom for all. Within a democracy there lurk
further obstacles related to the question of liberty. Compulsion, such
as military conscription, because of its incompatibility with individual
freedom of choice, represents a basic threat. The stock reply that
compulsion is just when it becomes necessary did not satisfy Maeztu.
It followed that laws were just when they were needed. But in asking
how many would be essential for the preservation of a society, he felt
that not many were. Nonetheless, even those democracies that pride
themselves on the extent of personal liberty granted citizens have had
to amend it so as to guard their own welfare. Thus England, nurtured

on Stuart Mill's liberal dicta, while preserving the rights of conscientious objectors, found herself establishing a wartime draft.

The specter of individual liberalism versus common-goal democracy is raised again when Maeztu denies the sufficiency of having a responsibility only to oneself and God, and not to one's fellow citizens, for in a democracy it is not enough to do one's duty but necessary to see that others do theirs as well. The most glaring shortcomings of a democracy devoid of compelling rules would be inefficiency and injustice. The coward would not have to bear arms, the avaricious would not have to pay taxes, and the lazy would not have to work. As Maeztu saw it, the supreme virtue of compulsion was forcing the undesirable citizen to work for the benefit of all. The voluntary principle, thought Maeztu, allowed the individual too much freedom. It permitted him to work but also gave him the right not to do anything if he so chose. In a system based on justice, everyone must be compelled to do work. Reiterating his disapproval of Mill's individual rights, he theorized that if societies were created solely to respect the individual's wishes, then democracies whose objective purported to be the realizing of ideals superior to the goals of the individual made no sense. Aware of its many pitfalls, democracy, a majority system, remained for Maeztu the form of political structure within which each citizen could enjoy the greatest latitude of personal freedom. At least in the kind of democracy he envisioned the serious injustices generated by the dastardly, the indolent, and the felon would not be among its drawbacks.

Maeztu questioned Mill's affirmation that personal liberty constitutes the best method to further intellectual progress. Maeztu brings out the evidence of organized thinking involved in the preparation for and conduct of war. Without it, submarine warfare, arms supply, coordinated attacks, and other aspects of the conflict would not have been possible. The same number of individuals laboring and thinking, not as a team but isolated from one another, would not have been as effective. And yet civilian or peacetime needs differ from military ones only in urgency. As industrial supremacy cannot be maintained lest new and better ways of production are discovered through tests in laboratories by research teams, i.e. organized thought. Admittedly, writes Maeztu, the surfacing of an isolated inventor is not so very uncommon yet it is almost always cause for surprise.

Mass man, the average man, in any society largely avoids thinking beyond a superficial stage because he finds it too hard. This is where

Mill was wrong according to Maeztu, for he believed that man only needed to be granted freedom in order to produce ideas beneficial to society. Instead Maeztu finds so great a resistance to this intellectual activity that even government has had to compel its citizenry if not to think, at least to engage in various intellectual operations through enforced schooling, literacy tests, etc. That governments have tried to quash intellectual activity is also true, but these efforts have nearly always met with failure. Bent on the idea of function, he considers individualized thought most inefficient for society's common good. He holds thought to be a key social function and as such one to be not only "acknowledged [but] organized" (172).

Maeztu has convinced himself that both authoritarian and liberal individualistic ordered societies constitute undesirable forms of government due to the principle of inviolable basic sovereignty—the State's and the individual's respectively—upon which they are both founded. The two opposites coincide at one point, however, because their moral is equally subjective and anthropocentric. The reasoning goes that a subjective morality is one in which someone determines the evil or goodness of an object. The object per se is neither good nor bad. Such subjectivism has prevailed since the Renaissance and from it an equally subjective political system derived subsequently, infused with an inner-directed morality. Liberals, like Stuart Mill, expectedly declared the individual to be the source of this sovereign morality while authoritarians, such as Hegel, spoke of the State as the supreme morality. In both schools of thought man, and not society, reigns as the source of a morality tautologically subjective. It is fortunate, then, that subjective morality, the source of authoritarian and liberal principles, has never had as great an impact on the masses as it did on intellectual circles.

Up to this point the adepts of Hegel had advocated an authority to make all the decisions in view of man's inability to deal with moral matters. The liberals, on the other hand, saw no point in coercive laws and sought complete personal freedom. But under the new ethic something else has been added or at least clarified: man is neither good nor bad, he is good only when he performs beneficial deeds, so that a good-doer may become evil whenever he acts wrongfully. Conversely, things are independent, their value does not change, according to Maeztu. Thus, the good act performed is superior to its executor. The change is radical: man is no longer the measure or the center of morality; it has been transposed to acts and objects. In this way secular humanism can be overcome. Morality's object, Maeztu now hopes, will no longer center on man's self-realization but instead on the preservation of power, knowledge, justice, and law, all of these representing the supreme good of society.

Maeztu, who had previously believed in an active dialectic between man and objects, no longer recognizes this relationship. For him just as truth exists independent of man, so good resides in things whether they better man or have no effect on him. The "neorealist ethic" translates essentially into the objective morality sought so desperately by Maeztu to oppose the subjective morality that breathed life into authoritarianism and liberalism. With it a new social theory is possible.

Considering that all societies are characterized by a common denominator, i.e., a goal sought by a majority of component members, Maeztu reasons that the object of this communal goal carries a positive intrinsic value. The goal, then, patently superior to all others including those represented by individuals, becomes by moral right the directing force. Society ordered in this fashion at the same time transcends and unites all individual interests. No one has more rights than the rest. Right would then become inextricably linked to function so that when performance of social functions ceases, the enjoyment of rights would be diminished proportionately. In this near utopia conceived by Maeztu, arguments concerning the power of the governor versus the rights of the citizen would disappear, there remaining only questions of jurisdiction since the performance of one's duty would constitute (and define) the extent of everyone's rights or privileges.

The ideal of every socialist party has been the society above outlined, one where economic, military, and political power is distributed among the various segments of society to individuals capable of fulfilling functions that allow for potential growth and development in each particular case. However, the socialist value system hardly differs, as Maeztu saw it, from that of conservative middle classes. The same utopia is sought by both, a situation where work hours diminish independently of pay increases in freely chosen occupations. Comfort becomes the ideal, "The greatest happiness of the greatest number" (185). But a man aspiring to nothing greater than material well-being certainly will never risk his life for, say, something as vague as a matter of justice. Hedonism thus prevents the working man from achieving his utilitarian ideal. In a society where justice is not the basic tenet, few workers can hope to overcome the odds in favor of the privileged classes. It remains for the socialists to realize that though their fondness for material comforts can remain, their goal must be something greater.

In seeking ways to convince the working classes that the ideals of Truth, Justice, Love and the existence of God are indispensable to life, Maeztu comes up with a belleletristic solution to be taken in earnest, the novel. He reasons that since the search for happiness, material or otherwise, does not constitute a logically demonstrable or attainable need, but instead a sentimental or imaginary one, novels seem eminently qualified as a means to this end. They can be looked upon as cathartic in the Aristotelean sense: purifiers. The reader identifies with the protagonist thus sharing his concerns, ambitions, successes, and disappointments. Reading allows man vicariously to experience perils, devoid of all danger. Drawing from George Meredith's *The Egoist,* and Miguel de Cervantes' *Don Quijote* as counterpoint, Maeztu illustrates in the first case how a self-seeking personality soon tires of the desired object and, in the second place, how even the most altruistic individual—Don Quijote—cannot find happiness no matter how dedicated his life may be. Just as the heroes of great literary masterpieces do not find happiness, man cannot hope to either. Pleasure entails grief whoever we are, whatever we do. Such is the lesson learned from the novel to be applied to life.

Maeztu points out the impossibility of a better world unless man looks beyond his pursuit of happiness. Man will neither make himself nor anyone else happy. It would be better to adopt socialism because as a system it incorporates a fundamental sense of justice, not because it holds the promise of attainable happiness. Followers of Hedonism will only discover with subsequent dismay the falseness of this ideal.

The socialist movement, driven not only by the ideal of justice but also by the pursuit of happiness, weakens itself by the incompatibility of the two. The proletariat, reasoned Maeztu, works now in order not to have to work later. Its real goal is freedom from toil, an essentially egotistic end. In order to attain a wish (in this case, idleness) one must first endure a disagreeable sensation—work. Evidently the relationship between action and desire is an inverse and not a direct one. Man's nature is characteristically a play of opposites, or to have his cake and eat it too, as Maeztu puts it.

Capitalism's failure can best be ascertained in the economic sphere, socialism's in the sociopolitical realm. World War I strained the social fabric not only by exacting a cost in human lives, but also in terms of shortages of goods, and in spiralling national debts. The ensuing peace did not mean as rapid a recovery as people had a right to expect due to the unequal control of wealth in capitalist nations. The monopolistic control of manufacturing and industry generated prolonged and, at times, artificial shortages. On the other side of the coin, in the instances where socialism was tried, it resulted in equal failure. The fault lay in the desire to combine a liberal attitude with the communist approach to the task at hand so that each individual had only to work to the best of his abilities, with himself as the sole judge of these. The result, Maeztu explains caustically, shows human nature's frailty in that the indolents' burden had to be borne by the industrious until these could no longer sustain the load. And yet examples abound where the communist system has worked unfalteringly for centuries. Religious communities, for one, are quite successful in spite of their communistic order of life, but only because the liberal aspects—unchecked personal freedom—have been extirpated. Discipline and rule, or distribution of work and organization, are the guidelines in their success.

Maeztu nevertheless does not advocate the breakup of society into numerous smaller communities, as John Ruskin and William Morris suggested in their advocacy of a return to the medieval system of artisans' guilds. Man needs machines even to farm, so that industry and large population centers are indispensable, but a combination of the two might produce a more just society. What Maeztu is calling for is guild socialism. Under such a system, work would not be a commodity at the disposal of the wealthy. Just as important, it would ensure the workers' participation in the decisions affecting production and controlling availability of needed goods so that shortages would occur only unintentionally and to no one's calculated benefit. This would be a long way from the earlier cited perils of both capitalism and socialism since the necessity to work for a living remains for everyone—Maeztu quotes *Genesis* (IV, 9), "In the sweat of thy face shalt thou eat bread" (169).

If the ideal of the pursuit of happiness proved vain, the ideal of luxury fared even worse in Maeztu's catalogue of social evils. As another lesson drawn from the war he noted how England, short-handed for the production of armaments, put together a work force made up of regular industrial personnel as well as individuals recruited from other trades ranging from domestic servants to professionals in nonessential industries. In this way the country more than met her needs and contributed to the winning of the war. Maeztu noticed, however, that even after the hostilities among nations ceased, shortages of essential goods kept cropping up due to employment of a great number of people in the production of needless and useless luxury items. The hands that ought to ensure a steady supply of items necessary for the nation's daily life instead provide superfluous commodities for the affluent.

Capitalism allows the production of luxury items to the detriment of the needs of the underprivileged. Maeztu denied the popularly held notion that since it is the working class who produces these unaffordables, it reaps certain benefits, a living wage. His answer is that the poor should not only derive a living, but a worker should do something meaningful as well as useful with his life. Better than a prostitute made comfortable by a rich man's lust would be no prostitute at all. A harvester is preferable to a diamond ring; the first one keeps providing work and benefit to many, the second merely adorns the hand of the idle with its sterile presence.

For Maeztu a postwar period does not differ significantly from the days of war. He sought a functional and efficient society where nothing is wasted and everything, and everyone, has a specific purpose or duty. He would forbid the production of luxury items with no one allowed to consume anything beyond what could be deemed necessary for the individual's welfare and his capacity to carry out his assigned social function. To whom the regulatory functions are to be entrusted Maeztu does not say, yet only the State would have the power to enforce such stringent laws. He entrusts, perhaps unconsciously, an increasing amount of authority to the government in an effort to realize his ideal society. In such an abdication lay the beginnings of his later totalitarian ideas that drove him to support the dictatorship of Miguel Primo de Rivera and to formulate the first pages of Spanish fascism.

Government was to have its finger in every pie. Maeztu despised especially capitalism's disposition for tilting the market in favor of the moneyed such as in the case of feigned shortages to drive up prices, and not being able to discern other means with which to check these inequities, he entrusted the State with the power to dictate equitable regulations.

As this section draws to a close, Maeztu sweeps across the centuries bringing forth the reasons why he believes man has failed in his quest to build a stable society. He has come full circle since "Liberty and Organization," the initial segment, dwelling once again upon man's supreme self-confidence and the resulting subjective social systems derived from the notion of unrestricted personal liberty. Voicing anew his desire for a society in which man's rights are founded solely on his function, Maeztu tolls the bell for Romanticism as the last and great age of egocentrism.

His concept of the Romantics derives from T. E. Hulme, his friend and sometime spiritual guide, according to whom the Romantics believed that man was innately good. Hulme, and then Maeztu, rejected this contention and tried their best to discredit it. In these pages, Emerson, Maeterlinck and Carlyle are the targets of his indignation. For these three Romantics man's greatness could be proven by his great works; in fact greatness could only be explained through man himself and not through his actions or words. Maeztu was convinced that man though capable of greatness was not innately great or even good.

His greatest bête noire, not unexpectely, was Jean Jacques Rousseau whose *Le Contrat social* did much to fuel the French Revolution. The treatise's first and perhaps most important sentence, "Man is born free but everywhere he is burdened with chains," could not be accepted by Maeztu who questioned the meaning of to be free or to be born free (188). There can be no rights without function for Maeztu. Man is entitled to what he produces, he does not even have the right to be free. Leibniz, the first of the idealist philosophers before Rousseau, is blamed for the spiritual optimism that encouraged man to think that he alone had the right to go his own way. And Kant, with his affirmation that goodness is not intrinsic to objects but a property of the observer when free, shares in the guilt. Maeztu saw Romanticism as a deceiver because it allowed man to think of himself as a king only to discover that he has no "throne," no basis for authority. When a cause is sought for its disappearance, the culprit turns out to be manifold, "society, the human body, the nature of the world" (190). It follows that to regain his "throne" man will wage war on the assumed usurpers. Romanticism, the offspring of Renaissance humanism, could only lead to ever-growing conflicts, ultimately the First World War.

A look at Classicism revealed to Maeztu much in common with Romanticism but with significant safeguards. Man might have been a king, nevertheless he was considered subservient to God. He had power over the world's creatures yet he felt bound to higher values and authority. Being human, man, though not altogether inferior, cannot pretend to control his own destiny. This essentially Christian attitude lay at the heart of Maeztu's vision for a future society, the recognition by man of his own limitations. This would rid him of his egoism and pride, and facilitate a new world order.

Maeztu writes that it is pure conjecture to hold that an individual is happiest when endowed with the liberty to act at will. Moreover the very existence of a society integrated by such privileged citizens would be in peril since man is wont to follow impossible notions. The concept of liberty itself, Maeztu felt, was misunderstood even by those who praised it. At the same time to deny man certain basic freedoms, such as the right to follow his professional vocation, would amount to the destruction of his will to function constructively. Maeztu admits that man is a free agent and not a machine, yet when he defends man's freedom of thought he is defending his *capacity* to think, not his *liberty* of thought—his thinking, not his liberty. Liberty, Maeztu goes on to say, "is not in itself a positive principle of social organization. . . . Liberty would constitute no society at all" (192). Better to fight for cherished goals rather than to achieve the same result in the name of freedom; instead of opposing a restrictive authority for liberty's sake, better to have waged war on authoritarianism for its own ills. As he had spoken of the failure of authority in the inaugural part of the book, Maeztu attaches the same stigma to liberty in this section. He is suspicious of man, believing that his arbitrary nature will lead him astray whether on the side of authority, by tyranny, or on the side of liberty, by the dissolution of society. As before, his one word with respect to both ends of the sociopolitical spectrum is *caution*. He would rather see too little liberty granted to man or State, rather than too much.

IV   *Function and Values*

In this third and last part of *The Crisis of Humanism* Maeztu outlines his plan for a stable society. Having dismissed the principles of authority and liberty, he looks to a mode of government that harmonizes the principle of justice with human needs and aspirations. The spirit of the guild institutions holds that promise.

An incident in wartime England, a strike declared by several trade unions as a protest against excessive profits by industrialists and owners, resurrected the guild spirit. Their protest came to the attention of Maeztu and his colleagues at *The New Age* magazine. They saw in this a renewal of guildism in that intended limitation of the power of the few constituted the main reason for the strike. Limitation and hierarchy had been the two guiding axioms of the guilds since their medieval inception. Limitation meant the right of an individual to receive payment in exchange for his work and, determined by his capabilities, a minimum as well as a maximum wage for everyone. By hierarchy, the guild understood the ranking of workers according to ability so that the apprentice, officer, and master titles suggested a proven proficiency.

The key to understanding Maeztu's idea of a new social order lies in his principles of individual rights according to function, and government decentralization. The guild system comes into play for distributing the State's power, not in the usual geographic sense of regions or provinces, but according to the principle of function. The State was to disperse the various functions to different guilds capable of fulfilling the task required.

The significant factors to keep in mind were the reasons why the guild system declined, in order to avoid the same pitfalls for the future. Among the most important failures had been the guilds' inability to gain fuller control of the cities and towns where they were established. Banking and commerce had not been regulated by guilds, a serious error since with the inflow of gold from the New World, power was concentrated under the control of very few individual autocrats. Finally, the lack of foresight to expand their control over the overseas colonies' tradesmen made it impossible for guilds at home to compete with cheaper imported products. Maeztu obviously thought these mistakes could and had to be avoided. That the guild institution might encounter completely new obstacles in a modern environment perhaps did not occur to him or at least did not concern him unduly. Yet this would be the greatest obstacle to the implementation of such an outmoded system.

In order for the guild spirit to triumph in the twentieth century, Maeztu believed that a sense of solidarity and cooperation had to surface among men. The World War, to his way of thinking, had done much to bring about that feeling. Wartime is a period when the extraordinary substitutes for the norm, privileged classes lose their exemptions, everything in fact unites for a common purpose. The armed forces become a guild where the whole nation joins during conflict. At no time is it truer that the differences between rich and poor disappear than in a wartime army. There one attains his rank by dint of his function and the ability with which it is discharged, a form of organization that coincides with the traditional guild system.

The war over, Europe suffered from many of the same ills as before the conflict. In fiscal terms, the situation was almost desperate. The economies of France, Italy, Belgium, and Rumania were near collapse, and it was an idle hope that Germany could subsidize war losses. The postwar shortages were due to the diversion of civilian attention from crop growing and production of staple goods to military enterprises. Yet one thing had changed in the years of war, the working classes became aware of common effort. To Maeztu it seemed inconceivable that poor people who had seen the rich share with them the burden of struggling for a national goal would now, at war's end, return to their familiar posts and bear alone the brunt of alleviating national crises. In the armed forces they had been rewarded equitably. Maeztu realized that the guild-like organization of society during war had been an imperious necessity, yet he wished that what had been done for expediency's sake having been found just, efficient, and satisfying to most would be continued when reason dictated its viability.

Maeztu wanted the notion of solidarity to become a reality, but in order to put it into practice, it first had to be made workable. Maeztu had found what he wanted for his "no function–no rights" society in the writings of the French political scientist Leon Dugit. This University of Bordeaux professor had substituted the objective concept of law for the traditional subjective concept of Roman law. For Dugit the code then governing Germany (the so-called "organic theory") was not acceptable since it could not be determined whether power lay in the hands of the State or in its members. This uncertainty left the State as the only source of power; it alone could pass and define laws, in other words, police itself. The representative system of government as practiced both in England and France did not satisfy him either.

Dugit's "doctrine of objective rights" rested on the belief that men live under a social rule, the basis for which is interdependence. This concept Maeztu purports to be self-evident, and he himself had advocated it in the past. He contended that the way society functions resembles a group of friends who wish to play football; the rules arise from the fact that the participants are interdependent, and no single individual has the subjective right to impose rules. Society's rules are established for the same reasons. The laws of conduct of necessity have to be the same for all. Accordingly, the principle of sovereignty, would disappear. To ensure the accountability of those in power, Dugit, as skeptical of man's goodwill as Maeztu, proposed the installation of a high court made up of representatives from each social class to pass judgment on the validity of the laws dictated.

Having found his ideal of solidarity theorized into a legal formulation, Maeztu now needed only to find a way to make it viable. His way would be to nurture the then current syndicalist movement, to organize all social strata so that none of them would have complete power over the others. Progressively the government's authority would diminish until its sole function would be that of arbiter and regulator. On a global scale Maeztu maintained that his objective theory ought to be the cornerstone of relations among nations. At this international level he began by recalling the universal hopes of a lasting peace following the four years of the largest-scale war the world had ever seen. The States' way to fulfill the expectations of their peoples consisted of a general policy of preserving a status quo in the world map. Maeztu's first objection was that the status quo, by definition static, completely disregards life and time's dynamic nature. The solidification of conditions as they existed would perpetuate inequality, an order as undesirable as war. Still more basic was Maeztu's denial of international law; as far as he was concerned, it did not exist.

The inspiration behind the League of Nations was Woodrow Wilson's belief that the preservation of extant conditions would ensure world security. It was constituted on the equally erroneous notion that nations of recognized sovereignty could form an association without losing that sovereignty but having it guaranteed by a higher authority, the League's own authority derived from the combined total of its members'. In Maeztu's view this meant that no such association could exist. When the object of the League of Nations became the preservation of its members' sovereignty, it followed that they could neither abdicate it nor delegate it even for the League's own survival. He perceives the error not in its having been founded on the basis of the nations' sovereignties but on a subjective concept of law: "What has failed . . . is law founded on sovereignty and consequently on the subjective conception of law" (226), a return once more to the essential thought that without function no right exists. This applies equally to the individual and the State: "To the objective doctrine of law the exclusive source of international law, as of private and public law, is function" (227). On a larger scale, again, it is no more difficult to force the State to comply than it is to force the individual; in order to be persuaded, both must be made to feel that worse things will result from a recalcitrant stance.

According to Maeztu's no functions–no rights objective theory, the sovereignty of the State is determined by its fulfillment of the "necessary functions for the conservation and increase of solidarity in the planet Earth and in cultural values" (228). From this principle he extracts norms to justify the primacy of the State. Three factors become the yardstick: 1) The openness of a nation with regard to free travel within and outside of its borders by both foreigners and natives. This would include not only protection for foreign travellers but also maintaining an adequate transportation network. 2) The State must exploit all the resources present within its territory for its own benefit but without monopolizing foodstuffs and raw materials needed by the rest of the world. 3) Every State would be compelled to look upon its own citizens as depositaries of cultural values and provide them with an education both to earn a living and to contribute to an increase of "the cultural goods of the world" (229).

There is no doubt in Maeztu's mind that the norms proposed would be most difficult to enforce, yet in passing judgment on a foreign State, they amount to the most objective set of standards possible. They constitute a set of rules on which to base international law, a means for a court, such as the League of Nations, to operate. The objections that can be made to this new basis for international law are many. The nations who stand to lose most from the reevaluation of these laws would surely refuse to accept the provisions. Maeztu felt all along, however, that fear of another world conflict constituted the greatest deterrent and would persuade the powerful and the not-so-powerful nations to accept the new order.

The objective concept of international law derives from the national social order where the different classes would be constituted into guilds committed to diminishing gradually the power of a central government. So the ability of national governments to resist the implementations of the objective principle seemed to Maeztu unlikely in view of what he felt was the resurgence of the guild system spirit. And yet he was no dreamer, because even though he would have preferred to think that rational arguments prevailed in favor of the desirability of the social order he advocated, Maeztu was sure that the horrors of the last war might probably be the reason why men would abandon the idea of sovereignty and accept an order of a different sort based on a "law founded on things" common to all mankind.

V   The Primacy of Things and Objective Rights

The "primacy of things" now emerges as one of the key theories toward which Maeztu has been leading. This formula synthesizes in the author's own words what *Authority, Liberty . . .* and *The Crisis of Humanism* have to say about morals, sociology and political science. Maeztu leaves no doubt but that the most important social principle is the thing or things, spiritual as well as material, in which men are united. The Church provides an example for him, appearing as an association founded on a thing, Christian dogma, that must be seen as its primary concern. The church edifice, the faithful, the clergy, and the liturgy are only secondary means to the principal end—dogma. The problem is, however, that once constituted, associations lose sight of the primacy of the thing that gave them birth and conflicts arise from questions of membership, jurisdiction, purpose, and means (the members) become more important than the end (the founding common goal).

Maeztu acknowledges that one obstacle to the acceptance of his primacy of things arises because of the notion that things, especially spiritual or abstract ones, exist with inherent values. People, for instance, become skeptical when told that if two persons love each other, the relationship involves something besides the lovers, a thing shared called Love. Even if things such as Love, Truth, Power, or Justice are acknowledged to exist, their independence from man is rarely conceded. Maeztu holds that their nature must be thought of as inherent and absolute. There is also relative value found in those things, actions, relations, and men touched by an absolute value. The reason men cannot be considered absolute values, inherently good, is man's capacity for evil. Thus man, alone or in association, must always remember the primacy of things above himself.

Clearly, Maeztu intends his formula to mean that man is obligated to serve absolute values—Justice, Power, Love, and Truth. These are above any institution, association, or even society and their need is universal in order to reach a superior goal. In this fashion, pragmatically, the doctrine of the primacy of things could begin to yield results. The conflict of the individual versus the State could not have been resolved until this point without raising the specter of tyranny, anarchy, or unionism. Now judgment can be rendered, taking into account the function of each contestant in light of the end pursued. Societal conflicts arise due to the jurisdictional crisscrossing brought about by the multiple memberships of each individual in associations (federal, state, county, and city taxpayer, resident, traveller, and so on) with overlapping interests. This occurs because "Law has not been based on the relation of the associated [individual(s)] with the *thing* that associates them; but has been sought to be founded directly on the associated themselves, independently on the thing associating them" (250). Contrary to this line of thought, Maeztu's idea of the primacy of things denies that any human rights are inherent; they are adherent for they occur only in function of something else. And so we are back to the no function-no rights principle.

Maeztu thinks it imperative to establish a society where social classes would be drawn according to their function: educators, farmers, scientists, artists, etc., and ranked according to their proficiency. This implies a constant reevaluation of everyone's performance and derived rights, something totally foreign to Maeztu's society at that time but a process that would doubtless raise its efficiency. More important, perhaps, it would ensure the right man the right job and reward his work accordingly.

In his advocacy of the primacy of things Maeztu tries to dislodge subjectivism from the rule of society. He is trying also to eradicate the liberal democratic notion that man is his own master who need not serve anyone but himself. Democracy for Maeztu cannot be real unless it has as its principal objective work for the common good "either spontaneously or through mutual coercion" (225). The true basis of democracy, in his view, ought to be that no man have any other rights than those he needs as "an instrument of eternal values" (255).

As he approaches the end, Maeztu begins to close the circle. Humanism and its last remnants once again become the target. Just as he had reversed Protagoras' dictum "Man is the measure of all things" into "Things . . . give us the measure of all men" (243) in his apologue for the primacy of things, he now calls for man to divest himself of anthropocentric pride and believe in a higher value than himself. Just as war exacts great sacrifice and produces irrational acts (heroism), so life under normal circumstances demands more than solely justice and other rational values. Peacetime had, according to Maeztu, lulled man into forgetting life's essentially tragic nature, scored by death and resurrection. Now whether man can be convinced and made aware of these inevitabilities through reason remains doubtful in Maeztu's mind; only through sentiment can it be communicated. Here faith comes into play, the altruistic need to sacrifice oneself for one's successors or for the welfare of society's future.

Maeztu suspects that man can be convinced that a society based on the principle of function is better than one founded on either the authority or the liberty principles because it is more just. The likelihood that he would choose such a social order rests on the realization that World War I had come about as a result of the antagonism between liberty and authority, both unequally unjust and disproportionally guilty of the conflict because of their foundation on subjective rights. Yet is it not enough to surrender one's rights in order to establish a society on a just principle, the need is for the sacrifice of one's own personality. The renunciation would amount to nothing short of death of the self because even if resurrection were assured, it would mean *apocatastasis*, the return of each individual to his origins as part of the great whole. This end, advocated by Maeztu as the supreme sacrifice of the ego for the benefit of the common good, was violently opposed by many of his contemporaries, loudest of all by Unamuno who resisted it even if it took the form of *anacefaleosis*, meaning the recapitulation of all creatures in Christ. Maeztu, however, felt that by man forsaking so much, humanism's egocentristic backbone could be broken and man once more become a "servant of the good" (268).

The doctrine of objective rights, contrary to what might be thought, does not carry a set scale of objective values, invariable for all societies and all ages alike. It does, nevertheless, demand one supreme value which could be anything from pleasure to piety, and that the laws governing that particular society maintain a vigil so that the chosen value is preserved and augmented. Those striving on its behalf, accomplishing a positive function, merit the rights, power, and wages; those standing idle, not fulfilling any function, receive no benefits of any sort. And finally, those bent on destroying or diminishing the chosen supreme value would be criminally punishable. A legislative branch would determine the hierarchies, rights accrued to every function, and the power due each functionary. The judicial board would also determine applicants' aptitudes for each given function. This represents for Maeztu a stopgap measure since, as lawyers and other professionals then judged the aptitude of their candidates, he meant for everyone else eventually to do the same. There would be exceptions, of course, such as a wealthy young man inheriting a vast amount of money. Labelling it subjective right—a privilege—Maeztu would have the heir demonstrate his financial know-how prior to receiving the wealth.

Maeztu entertained great hopes for his function principle as a basis for a new society. As a beginning it would be enough for the controllers of public opinion—"politicians, professors, publicists" (270)—to embrace the principle, something he believed they would do if its expediency and its justice were proven. Both attributes have been dealt with at some length in previous pages, nevertheless Maeztu marshals his arguments anew synthesizing all we have learned from the very beginning.

The quality of justice appears most evident since the system working on a function principle confers rights solely on those individuals, regardless of birth, race, or social status, capable of and willing to execute their chosen or assigned function. Its practicability is demonstrated by Maeztu's proof of the failures of societies based on subjective rights, whose worst shortcoming is a tendency to boundlessness. From the Renaissance onward it had been considered man's right to develop his personality without limitation. The discovery of the Americas gave impetus to this tendency to reach for the infinite, yet as the world progressively shrank with increased millions of inhabitants, limits had to be established. Resources were not endless after all. So the subjective principle had to be amended repeatedly. The most logical course of modification would be to base rights on the principle of function, so that security and sufficiency could be ensured since only the necessary space and rights proportionate to the function entrusted would be forthcoming.

Although Maeztu observed that the doctrine of objective rights does not call for a specific table of values, he has embraced a set throughout the length of *Authority, Liberty* . . . and *The Crisis of Humanism* that in his mind are the only universal ones with intrinisic value: Power, Truth, Justice, and Love. The four he felt were irreducible and considered them God's own attributes. Based on these supreme values, Maeztu proposed a new philosophy with branch disciplines to substitute for traditional logic, ethics, and aesthetics, which would be law (science of justice), cratology (science of power), erotica (science of love), and logic (science of truth). Man, he considered an instrumental value. If he acted in accordance with universal values, then he possessed an adherent value, as opposed to the inherent quality of the universal or supreme values. Man could not single out and pursue only one of these values without turning his back on the rest, and yet not all of them could be reached in unison. The dilemma can be solved, Maeztu realized, if each of the other absolute values becomes the instrument with which to realize the rest. The ideal in a society based on these universal values would be harmony between them, but no guarantee exists that conflicts would not surface. Maeztu understood this and, confessing that an abstract scale of values would not suffice where even the *Decalogue* can only offer general guidance, he asserted one last time that every man's duty, i.e. function, is to work to make the above values a part of this world.

VI   *The Final Plea*

In summary, Maeztu produces four decisive arguments that he feels will incline mankind to build future societies on the function principle.[6] Foremost in his mind is the need to find a superior principle that will check the characteristic excesses of authority. The liberal principle cannot be used since its adoption in place of authoritarianism would only lead to a society lacking solidarity. War could never be fought under a liberal banner since it would entail a common goal, something incompatible with the doctrine of liberalism which guarantees absolute personal freedom. If liberalism opted for its own preservation, it would perforce turn to authoritarianism in order to wage war effectively. We have then a vicious circle.

In favor of the function principle is its just nature. Under this principle no one has any rights which he does not deserve as evidenced in his ability to perform a function or service. The no function-no rights principle applies equally to the State's sovereignty as it does to an association's or an individual's rights.

The third argument involves the progress of syndicalism, the movement through which men choose to group themselves according to the functions they discharge, such as labor unions, medical associations, etc. In this way men acquire certain rights as a direct result of their function. The function principle sanctions every activity and rewards it with rights, their denial resulting only if man chooses not to function. If this unionism trend were to continue, then one day it would include nearly every member of society. At this point, society as a whole could demand a justification for some of the activities pursued. Only those guilds that produced a needed function would be rewarded, doctors, educators, farmers, manufacturers of staple goods, etc.; whereas the claim of the wealthy, the indolent or the criminal, unsupported by any useful functions, would be rejected.

The fourth reason for Maeztu's guarded optimism for the success of the function principle stems from the horrors of the World War just ended. Without the warning inherent in such destruction, man probably would not search for an alternative form of government. It is much simpler to organize a society on the principles of authority or liberty than on function, for the latter involves a never-ending process of gauging of ability and performance. Although the inclination remains, therefore, to keep the old systems, the memory of the war unleashed as a result of the incompatibility between the former political and social orders will hopefully prove to be more persuasive.

Retrospectively, Maeztu's warnings were all too accurate; the authority principle generated nearly half a century of fascism in Spain, and its clash with the principle of liberty brought about the Second World War. On the other side of the coin, however, his function principle where adopted has produced equally discouraging results; one need only cast a glance at bankrupt England.

Maeztu was too optimistic in his reading of man's inclination toward good, and though his advocacy for a society founded on a principle as equitable as function remains valid, existentialist skepticism precludes such a utopia in spite of the most lethal danger confronting mankind since its origins—World War Three.

CHAPTER 5

Maeztu's Trinity: Love, Power, and Wisdom

IN the summer of 1925 Ramiro de Maeztu taught at Middlebury College in Vermont. His lectures focused on selected topics of Spanish civilization, the great painters, El Greco, Velázquez, Goya, and literary figures such as Celestina, Don Quijote and Don Juan. In October, one month following his return to Spain, a new book of his was published under the title, *Don Quijote, Don Juan y la Celestina*. It turned out to be Maeztu's most important work in the realm of literature, the only one dealing exclusively with literary subjects, though again it contained little that was new. The volume was dedicated to Ezequiel P. Paz, editor of the Buenos Aires daily *La Prensa*, where most of the essays in the book had already appeared.

Almost since 1900 Maeztu had been concerned with these three themes, especially Don Quijote, in lectures and journalistic articles. Now, in 1925, he felt that his dispersed ideas were worth rescuing from the forgotten pages where they had initially appeared. To this end he reworked most of the essays striving to endow the collection with harmony and unity. In the Madrid daily *El Sol* (10/20/29) he wrote "What impelled me to take the trouble, essentially unproductive, of unifying into a book these essays is the conviction that they could attest to a very old truth: that a legend is more real than history; and a modern truth: that man's innermost secret, his recondite will is revealed in his dreams. It occurred to me that the supreme fruit of the imagination has to be found in the literary myths, and that the greatest literary myths of modern times are Don Quijote, Don Juan and Celestina, Spanish all three."[1]

These three myths, to which Maeztu will feel an allegiance up to

97

and including his late *Defensa de la Hispanidad*, 1934 (*In Defense of Hispanism*), are a tripartite ensemble: Don Quijote is love; Don Juan, power; and Celestina represents wisdom. They symbolize, in *Don Quijote, Don Juan y la Celestina*, the greatness as well as the decadence of the culture and the spirit of the Spanish people.[2] The personified human values embodied in the three figures give way, in Maeztu's interpretation, to moral dilemmas upon which he focuses his criticism. It is also a medieval Christian image, doubtless a reflection of the Holy Trinity recorded by Dante Alighieri, "Fecerni la divina *Potestade*/la somma *Sapienza*, e il primo *Amore*" (*La Divina Commedia*, "Inferno," Canto III) which constituted Maeztu's trilogy of leitmotifs.

The main purpose is to demonstrate that love is nothing without power and wisdom, power is nothing without love and wisdom, nor is wisdom anything without the other two attributes.[3] This synthesis, which at times may seem forced, weighs literature in terms of human realities. The three long essays, corresponding to the literary themes aforementioned, study each topic from the standpoint of its moral, social, and political significance. Maeztu's literary sensibility results in an extrinsic interpretation of what he calls great literary myths. Not all three essays, however, deal equally with the subject announced, the first deals with *Don Quijote* the novel and less with its protagonist; the second treatise deals with the character Don Juan Tenorio almost independently of Tirso or Zorrilla; and the last focuses its attention on Celestina, the personnage. The reason for such disparity can be found in the differing degrees of autonomy Maeztu finds the characters possess with respect to the literary work per se.

I   Don Quijote or Love

The tricentennial of the *Quijote's* (1605–1615) publication fell in those years of darkness for Spain following her defeat at the hands of the United States. The men most affected by this curious literary and historical happenstance were the members of the Generation of 1898 and their followers. Miguel de Unamuno wrote the *Vida de don Quijote y Sancho* (*Life of don Quijote and Sancho*) in 1905, and in that same year Azorín published his *La ruta de don Quijote* (*Don Quijote's Itinerary*), and Navarro Ledesma, *El ingenioso hidalgo Miguel de Cervantes Saavedra* (*The Ingenious Squire Miguel de Cervantes Saavedra*). Within ten years Ortega y Gasset wrote *Meditaciones del Quijote*, 1914 (*Meditations upon the Quijote*), Salvador de Madariaga, *Guía del lector del Quijote*, (*Guide for the Quijote's*

Reader), and Américo Castro his *El pensamiento de Cervantes (Cervantes' Thought)*, both in 1925. Without exception, none of these treatises deals strictly or even predominantly with literary aspects of Cervantes' masterpiece. Castro comes closer than any of them. Unamuno's interpretation, extremely subjective, is tinged with affective religiosity; Azorín's (he later wrote *Con Cervantes* [*With Cervantes*] and *Con permiso de los cervantistas* [*Begging the Pardon of Cervantine Critics*], in 1947 and 1948 respectively) represents an impressionistic appreciation of the countryside and wanderings of the knight; Navarro Ledesma's contribution amounts to a fictive biography of Cervantes treated as if he were a knight; Ortega's book views the *Quijote* as the genesis for the novelistic genre; and Madariaga's, much influenced by Unamuno, contributes incisive psychological guidelines toward the understanding of the masterpiece.

Although the established date of publication for Maeztu's *Don Quijote, Don Juan and la Celestina* is 1926, both his and Madariaga's books appeared in Madrid's bookstores at the same time at the end of 1925. The two works also had their journalistic origins in common, which afflicted Azorín's *Don Quijote's Itinerary* as well. Maeztu's was different, however, in that he concentrated his efforts on the novel, *Don Quijote*; the rest chose to pay closer attention to Don Quijote, the character. But without fail all betrayed a sense of disillusionment as a result of Spain's downfall.[4]

For a period of twenty-five years Maeztu had been developing his thesis about the *Quijote*. Amidst considerable shouting and booing from a disapproving crowd, in 1900, Maeztu delivered a lecture in Madrid's Ateneo, the capital's official literary meeting hall, proclaiming the novel's essentially decadent character for the first time. Scarcely a year later, in the daily *La Correspondencia de España* his name appeared below an article entitled "A Book for Old Folks" in which he reaffirmed his stance that the *Quijote* should not be read by young people who would be affected by its tone of disillusionment and capitulation. Many lectures and essays followed, including one opposing the 1905 celebration of the work's tricentennial anniversary. There came another "Decadence and the *Quijote*" (*El Sol*, May 27, 1926) summarizing his criticism of Cervantes' work, and defending his own book just published on the subject. The last reference to the *Quijote* made by Maeztu appeared in the Buenos Aires daily, *La Prensa*, "La incomprensión del Quijote" ("The Misunderstanding of the Quijote"). Throughout, Gonzalo Sobejano[5] argues persuasively,

Maeztu's Nietzschean bent is at work, those books written during periods of splendor such as Homer's *Odyssey* or Goethe's *Faust* are full of celebration and hope, while Cervantes' *Quijote*, conceived at a time of decline, drips with sorrow. "Art—advises Maeztu echoing Nietzsche's dictum—must be seen through the optics of life."[6]

The purely literary or aesthetic aspects of the *Quijote* do not interest Maeztu; he looks instead at the social, political, and moral questions arising from it. He offers an original historical interpretation welded to the country's *circumstancia*, remarkably similar in its crisis of decline to the period when Cervantes lived and wrote. There are no footnotes; quotes, judging by the number of errors, appear to be given from memory; and erudition gives way to persuasive and emotional arguments in favor of a strictly humanistic approach.

"Don Quijote or Love" is subdivided into seven essays: "Fiestas y decadencia" ("Celebration and Decline"), "Hamlet y Don Quijote" ("Hamlet and Don Quijote"), "La Vida de Cervantes" ("Cervantes' Life"), "La España de Cervantes" ("Cervantes' Spain"), "La concepción de Don Quijote" ("The Conception of Don Quijote"), "Los críticos del *Quijote*" ("The Critics of the *Quijote*"), "España y el *Quijote*" ("Spain and the *Quijote*"). These betray *ab initio* their journalistic origins and, by their respective titles, the nature of their content.

The initial essay looks back to 1905 when Maeztu had declared himself opposed to a national commemoration in honor of the *Quijote*, believing then than Spain best forget a work which symbolized her decadence. Carefully, he now declares the book's "decadence" to refer solely to its historical circumstance, signifying neither an aesthetic nor an ethic qualification.[7] For some members of the Generation of 1898, Spain's decline began as far back as the seventeenth century, and Maeztu takes Cervantes' *Quijote* as proof of this attitude. He viewed it as a book written by a tired man in a time when his country lay exhausted by the efforts of conquest and prolonged wars. In *Don Quijote* he consequently sees a hero whose exalted values are no match for his weary frame; "quiere, pero no puede" ("he wants to, but he can't") Maeztu writes on page 72.[8] It becomes a parody of the books of chivalry.

Maeztu does not admit to esoteric interpretations of the work, maintaining that the correct approach is one of humility and simplicity because it will place the reader on a level with its author and its protagonist. And only in that position can one fully understand the melancholy and disillusionment that pervade the book. Its merit as the swan song that underscored the inescapable decline of a nation, however, should preclude it from being read at the wrong time in life by those who would be adversely affected by its dejection and weariness. He believed it was a book written about, by, and for tired people at an age of decline, and what Spain needed now was an awakening of ideals.

Ivan S. Turgenev (1818–1883) was probably the first writer of stature to draw a parallel between William Shakespeare's Hamlet and Cervantes' knight of La Mancha. His much-cited study was translated into Spanish and published by the *Revista Contemporánea* of Madrid in 1879. Maeztu knew it well and profited from Turgenev's lesson. The similarities discovered by the latter refer to the works (date of publication of the novel and first staging of the play are both 1605), the protagonists' contrasting characteristics, and to the authors themselves, who died in 1616. Taking as his starting point the Russian's idealistic and romantic interpretation (which sees Hamlet as the irresolute and Don Quijote as the impatient aspect of human nature), Maeztu proceeds to elaborate on what he imagines were the emotions awakened by the two characters in the seventeenth century.

His premise is that Shakespeare and Cervantes wrote their works *Hamlet* and *Don Quijote* against Hamlet and Don Quijote. The two heroes are endowed with such one-sided, deficient personalities that the need for either spectator or reader complementary reaction cries out. Hamlet's tragic flaw lies in a meditative nature that forecloses any disposition toward an act which must be carried out to avenge one murder and avert others. The audience recognizes impatiently such a need and will demand it of the character. Don Quijote's flaw, on the other hand, results from his penchant for action without deliberation. In Don Quijote's case the reader secretly, but vehemently, wishes for the knight's return to the safety of his placid home and the company of his friends. He is not up to his feats; Hamlet is incapable of any.

Parts three and five are linked by the insistence on identification between the novelist and his fictional character. Maeztu was not the first to treat the theme; Navarro Ledesma had done it earlier in his already mentioned *The Life of the Ingenious Squire Miguel de Cervantes Saavedra* (1905), a work of considerable fictional appeal. Maeztu's quick biographical sketch of Cervantes reveals little except misfortunes and disappointments. Cervantes' career as a soldier began at age 24 in the naval battle of Lepanto where he lost the use of his left hand, and ended ten years later when he was ransomed, after

five of imprisonment, from the hands of Algerian pirates. His reward
for a decade of service to Spain was a menial commission that forced
him to withdraw in bitterness from government service. In his early
forties Cervantes entered business, floundering almost immediately
as a purveyor of supplies destined for the ill-fated Armada put
together by Phillip II. Next he succeeded in being named revenue
agent for Granada where his duties involved collecting overdue taxes.
Bad luck struck once more, with the loss of large sums of money he
had deposited for safekeeping in a Portuguese bank that went under
in 1595. Held personally responsible, Cervantes fought the Treasury
Department, until in September 1597, unable to win his case in
court, and penniless, he was imprisoned in Seville. Cervantes' first
novel, a pastoral potboiler, having been ignored, he tried his hand at
playwriting, only to be outdone by Lope de Vega, considered a
genius in his day, and his followers. The poetry he wrote was scarcely
better received and even less well remunerated. Cervantes found he
could not live by the pen. At the Seville jail a fifty-year-old man, a
failure as a soldier, as a businessman, as a dramatist, and as a poet,
began writing the story of a fifty-year-old knight who, oblivious to his
frailty, intended to right his country's wrongs.

Maeztu interprets Cervantes' purpose in writing his masterpiece
as showing the madness and the futility of placing one's dreams
beyond any means of attaining them. Cervantes no longer expected
anything from life, but he continued to believe in the ideals for which
Don Quijote fights. There is no resentment against society in the
Quijote, only an unreeling of the failures that result when a tired old
man, endowed with a spirit much younger than his body, ignores his
age and follows his idealism. His impotence, a result of such an
imbalance; his madness, a result of his convictions; and his comicity, a
result of his failures, symbolize a nation which though exhausted from
colonization and conquest, still wishes to pursue the idealistic course
of the past. Laudable though such an intent may be, it is doomed to
failure—wars cannot be fought without strong men, rich treasure, or
ample supplies. Spain in the Golden Age (1500–1700) had lost two
million men out of a total population of twenty-one million, her gold
had long ago been taken over by German banking houses and her
agriculture abandoned. Cervantes' personal and Spain's historical
decadence are one. In Maeztu's interpretation, as Cervantes himself
rests, he tells the readers of his Don Quijote, the Spaniards of his
time: "The world is haywire, neither you nor I can fix it. Wouldn't it
be better to adapt ourselves to its reality than to dream about
changing it, and to be saddened because it will remain the same?"

(57). The impact of such a conclusion, Maeztu contends, must not damage the strength of the young, capable in mind and in body of fighting for the resurgence of their country.

The sympathy that Don Quijote inspires, in spite of his ridiculous misadventures, is because he makes incarnate a cosmic and selfless love. He gives of himself without a thought for the sake of many who only scorned and laughed at his failures. This serves Maeztu to point to the dangers of quixotic behavior: "Let's not be Quijotes. He who becomes a redeemer ends up crucified" (67). Echoing the spirit of the Generation of 1898, especially Unamuno's, Maeztu states that although contemporary Spain needed a quixotic spirit again after having "rested" for almost three centuries, the country had to divest itself of Don Quijote's madness which was to venture out only on the strength of his love without the power or the wisdom essential to the success of his enterprise.

II *Don Juan or Power*

Six essays make up the second and shortest part of the book. They are: "El tipo de Don Juan" ("The Character of Don Juan"), "El españolismo de Don Juan" ("The Spanish Nature of Don Juan"), "El mito de Don Juan" ("The Don Juan Myth"), "El drama de Don Juan" ("Don Juan's Dilemma"), "La hora de Don Juan" ("Don Juan's Time"), and "La razón de Don Juan" ("Don Juan's Right"). Because these uniformly short pieces were written at different times, many arguments are repeated and transformed, yet their intent and meaning remain constant.

Don Juan has captivated the fantasy of more people than any other personnage in all of the world's literatures. The character's viability from his inception at the pen of a seventeenth century Mercedarian friar, Tirso de Molina (Gabriel Téllez's pseudonym), up to this very day remains unequalled. France, Italy, England, Germany all have their versions, both as the fictional hero of plays, poems, operas, and tales, and as the subject of innumerable critical studies, but Spain's claim to Don Juan's essential character can hardly be disputed. The acceptance of his very name, unchanged in its Castilian form no matter where it appears, attests to his Spanish origin. Every year in early November, on the eve of All Soul's Day, the theaters of every major city in Spain are packed with people who go to see the daring, irreverent, and amorous adventures of their literary hero.

For Maeztu, Don Juan, when viewed as a universal character, vanishes into a mere shadow and any effort to define him fails miserably. Maeztu prefers to distinguish between two basic types of

Don Juan, a north European and a Spanish Don Juan. The former is a brave soul filled with love and vainly searching the world over for the ideal woman. Yet every woman he encounters he finds unworthy of his sentiments because she refuses in her egotism to give herself wholly to him. His search for happiness results in bitter disappointment proportionate to the eagerness with which he pursues the elusive ideal woman. On the other hand, the Spanish Don Juan seeks not happiness but only momentary pleasure. He is not even in love; a Don Juan in love ceases to be himself. He is not a lover but a deceiver, a trickster of love. An absence of superior ideals distinguishes him from the Northern Don Juan. This lack shared by Spaniards in general accounts for the sympathy he arouses in his countrymen and for the inability of idealistic northern Europeans (for Maeztu, every country except his own) to understand his character. This is further proof of Don Juan's native "españolismo" ("Spanishness") for Maeztu, who feels that the troublemaker would be "deported" by countries now claiming him as theirs if they only knew his true identity.

Maeztu's arguments in favor of Don Juan's Spanish origins are not overly compelling, but, added to an already voluminous critical consensus and a widely held folkloric notion, there remains little to favor the opposite view. Maeztu, having dispensed to his own satisfaction of the question of national identity, proceeds as though the matter would never come up again until northern Europe created a viable Don Juan of its own. For now and for centuries past Spain's was the only genuine Don Juan—the rest, pale and inconsistent imitations.

Don Juan is in fact a myth made up of several legends: 1) the story of the rogue who squanders his life and fortune chasing after women, gambling recklessly; 2) the account of the inebriated young nobleman who, chancing upon a skull on his way home late one evening, kicks it as though it were a ball, and invites it to dinner; 3) the Gallegan custom of placing a service at supper for a deceased member of the family on certain days of the year, stemming from the ancient ritual of having dinner in church on All Soul's Day surrounded by the tombs of friends and family; 4) the Catholic belief that repentance at the end of a dissipated life ensures forgiveness; and 5) the archetypal female romantic figure who is pure, passionate, and devout all at the same time. Essentially these are the prime materials which integrate the Don Juan drama of the two greatest Spanish playwrights of the series: Tirso de Molina (1571?–1648) and José Zorilla (1817–1893).

Tirso's *El Burlador de Sevilla y Convidado de Piedra* (*The Deceiver of Seville and the Stone Guest*, 1630) was written by a member of a religious order at the time of the Counterreformation. It was a piece of moral import, eternal punishment commensurate with a life punctuated by two egotistic considerations, "Esta noche he de gozalla" ("Tonight I must have her") and "Tan largo me lo fiáis" ("I have plenty of time left [to repent]"). Zorilla's *Don Juan Tenorio* (1844) marks the beginning of the decline of Romanticism. The religious import is no longer paramount even if the subtitle reads "Drama Religioso-Fantástico en dos partes" ("Religious-Fantastic Drama in Two Parts"). Love becomes the dominant theme, a love so strong that it transforms the implacable justice of Tirso's God into the merciful forgiveness of Zorilla's. Doña Ines' intercession suffices to save her lover from damnation in Hell. Maeztu understands the mythical nature of the figure, but believes that most of his qualities can be embodied by real people.

Don Juan enamors many women, makes love to them, and yet he himself does not fall in love with any. If he were to do so, he would cease to be himself. This immunity to love makes him a formidable adversary; women cannot entrap him, and in his rivalry with other men he can move from one conquest to the next without a backward glance.

His fascination stems principally from the inexhaustible energy he possesses. Don Juan leads the life of a libertine and yet he does not grow the weaker for it. He is unchanging because he is inhuman; he cannot get ill from drink, nor fat from food, nor fatigued from succeeding escapades. Maeztu sees him as the masculine counterpart of "those fabulous queens of legend who would have their lovers of one night decapitated at dawn" (94). Furthermore, Don Juan is profligate yet he never runs out of money. In his limitless lust for freedom he does as he pleases, following only an undisciplined individualism. His instinct dominates over reason. He is his own law, and has an egotism so exaggerated that arrogance together with unbridled sensualism are his most recognizable traits. His strength derives from these two qualities. When he invites the statue of the Comendador Gonzalo de Ulloa to dinner, the reason is not skepticism but arrogance. It is a dare, a gesture that makes him attractive for his boldness. This same undisciplined will lead Don Juan to disobey his king while remaining loyal to him and recognizing his authority. He is not an outcast. When he fights in a war on the side of his country, his motives and Spain's do not coincide because Don Juan seeks the thrill of personal victory, though he gladly puts his sword at the service of his king.

Just as Don Juan remains loyal to a temporal authority, his

acknowledgment of God cannot be questioned. He blasphemes against the Church, the Saints, and God; he is a sinner; but a believer nevertheless. Indeed, Don Juan goes to hell in Tirso's drama for the very reason that he so believes in God's mercy that he overestimates it, certain that he has plenty of time to repent. He never doubts God's omnipotence; he simply is too confident in His forgiveness and lets himself be pulled down into the fires of hell by the death grip of the Comendador's statue. Tirso, mindful of the theological implications of his play (eternal damnation as a result of an abuse of confidence of God's mercy) was later to write another drama where the protagonist is condemned to hell for exactly the opposite reason—that he does not have enough faith in God's mercy. What makes Zorrilla's play attractive, aside from the romantic solution to a moral question, is that one can be as perverse as one pleases because God's infinite mercy and the pure love of some bride will save the wicked soul.

Don Juan is accepted, envied, and emulated because, despite his monstrous faults, he remains believable within the bounds of society's outer limits. He may be a rebel, but he is loyal to his king; he may scoff at the Church, but he believes in God; he may seduce women, but they love it; he may gamble, but he doesn't care whether he wins or loses; he may fight endless duels, but he is never defeated; he may drink to excess, but he is not overcome by wine. Don Juan is power incarnate, and power is a positive force. He misuses it, but he has it to squander as he pleases. Even Maeztu admires Don Juan for this reason. Don Juan's faults are grave but on the positive side; he is no murderer, robber, rapist, traitor, coward, or alcoholic. Maeztu sees in Don Juan a personality who successfully overcomes justice (Dike), reason (Logos), and fate (Moira) and achieves a level of absolute freedom that however unattainable in reality paradoxically seduces even the sanest of men.

It is true that Don Juan exists without any other ideal than to satisfy his own appetites, but the character's energetic indifference to good and evil in a race to assert his individualism is something Maeztu can appreciate. The will to power, a Nietzschean concept Maeztu hasn't forgotten,[9] at the service of superior ideals would, in his eyes, do much to enhance Spain's revitalization. The energy of Don Juan is to be coveted in light of its boundlessness. Yet power without ideals can be as useless as the latter without the former, a situation Maeztu thought characterized Spaniards of his time. Endowed with limitless personal power, Don Juan stood as a myth which, if interpreted as a source of power, had every reason for existing and was worthy of being believed in.

III   La Celestina *or Wisdom*

Comedia de Calisto y Melibea (*Drama of Calisto and Melibea*) was the original and complete title under which a play appeared in Burgos in 1499 that subsequently would popularly be known the world over as *La Celestina*. The change was due to the arresting force personified in the character of Celestina, whose name in time became part of the Spanish vocabulary meaning go-between or procuress. The tragicomedy, as it was labelled in its second edition (Seville, 1502), presents the love story of Calisto, a wealthy young nobleman ardent enough to enlist the aid of a go-between named Celestina, and Melibea. The go-between succeeds in her mission of delivering the reluctant and virginal heroine to Calisto for which she receives a gold necklace as payment. Unwilling to share this reward with her accomplices, Pármeno and Sempronio (Calisto's servants), Celestina is killed by them, and they are hanged. The three deaths are followed by Calisto's when he accidentally falls from a ladder used to enter his beloved's garden. Melibea, disconsolate at her lover's fate, takes her own life, thus ending the fatalistic work where greed and passionate love drive the major characters to their own demise.

Maeztu's essays are an interpretative, sociopsychological analysis of the play with particular focus on Celestina. It is this character's personality and not the drama as such that interests him. The struggle between Melibea's will to behave as a well-bred noblewoman and a natural bent to give in to love's promise is the initial contest for Celestina, who conceives of the difference between wenches and damsels as lying in the latter's concealment of love's rapture underneath an immutable exterior. Her psychological acumen must be directed, then, toward changing Melibea's proper disposition, by pleading (on behalf of Calisto) not for love's but for mercy's sake. Melibea could never accept, under the courtly love topos,[10] such a naked approach. Instead, she hears of Calisto's suffering (a literal aching that she understandably translates into a figurative one) from a toothache, and that only a prayer she knows well, plus her belt which has touched the holy places in Rome and Jerusalem, can cure him (a credible excuse). Melibea's initial resistance to Calisto's plaints changes, for now she is being asked to perform a charitable act. Outwardly this is not giving in to lust or weakness, but being generous and compassionate in helping to relieve someone else's ills. In this way Melibea no longer has to deny herself thoughts or talk of Calisto with whom she is smitten.

It takes Melibea only one day and one night to give in fully to her passion. Her life's course runs parallel to Calisto's in this regard: both are unable to sleep, without desire to eat or rest, alternately euphoric and depressed. When he sets eyes on her, he regards Melibea as a revelation of God's greatness. It is characteristic of the passion that seizes Calisto that she takes the place of religious sentiment in his soul. "I? I am Melibean, I adore Melibea, believe in Melibea and love Melibea" (114). With these two lovers, it is love itself that separates them from the rest of the world. Calisto and Melibea's love is like the love of God, and they would have to have been of His nature in order to satisfy it. Maeztu contends that it is not difficult to see how, had Romeo and Juliet not met their ill fortune so soon, they would have adjusted to marriage lasting till their natural deaths; yet Calisto and Melibea could never have endured married life once each discovered the other was not as much as they had imagined, each believing the other to surpass mortal nature.

Whereas Romeo's love for Juliet, and Dante's for Beatrice, developed because lover and beloved were alike and in their affinity exalted and strengthened each other, Calisto and Melibea love one another because they are opposites. He is a mystic, a man who confuses divine love with carnal love. She is a woman incapable of giving a look that does not offer in it all of herself. His mysticism and her sensuality together lend credence to the platonic legend of an ancient third sex, Maeztu reminds us, a creature with four arms, four legs, and two faces, so cunning and powerful that the gods, jealous of its prowess, cut it in two. Since that time both halves have sought to rejoin and gain their former awesomeness. While discounting the fable, Maeztu believes that within every man there exists a carnal and a spiritual self and that a harmony has to be struck between the two. This peace must come from within; to look for it outside oneself foreshadows a predictable failure. This occurs when Calisto and Melibea, unwilling to look inward, seek to find in each other that harmonious state. Every critic perceives Rojas' conception of love to be a negative one. For the tragedian, love constitutes a malevolent sentiment which engenders evil and destruction in those unfortunate enough to be its target.

Even if *La Celestina* had been conceived with an exemplary purpose in mind, as its subtitle announces, it is more probable the play's autonomy as a fictional or real account which its author felt compelled to relate, in Maeztu's words, "simply because it had impressed him so" (123). All of which does not preclude the tragicomedy's ethical foundations. As an esthetic solution, Maeztu believes every masterpiece involves a moral question. "Love is a misfortune" constitutes this work's primary moral concern. Rojas is referring to carnal love, the kind in which everyone and everything are excluded by the lovers—an egoism so total that in their passion they become oblivious to heaven and earth. Love of this sort results in a contradiction since each being is inextricably a part of his circumstance, aspiring to an impossibility that cannot be realized save in death where all ties are cancelled, and the individual for once is alone. The graveyard, concludes Maeztu, is the only garden where two lovers can truly be alone.

Like Juan de Valdés, Juan Valera, and Azorín before him, Maeztu cannot resist the temptation of rewriting Rojas' play, using the well-defined characters but having them act out a situation where they are man and wife. However, as pointed out above, Maeztu does not believe that happiness would have been possible for the two lovers. In Maeztu's re-creation (a three and one-half page narrative), Celestina and the two servants are dead as in the original work. A year later, Calisto idolizes Melibea, now his wife, even more than at first. They have not been apart from each other for those twelve months. He cannot tear himself away from her though at times he seems to realize that life passes by, and he is being left behind without accomplishing anything significant. Calisto grows progressively weaker and more pale while Melibea's beauty and strength increase perceptibly. Maeztu ends the parody at this point, saying that in a bitter cold winter the archives of city hall were used as heating fuel and thus the story's end cannot be known, though he adds that some people have said that Calisto finally went completely mad with love, while others tell how he joined a military expedition, and still others confess to having seen him pray in church while, outside, Melibea smiled fondly at a courtly gentleman. That the tragicomedy could have only ended in such a fashion explains why Rojas had the good sense to end it as he did, contends Maeztu. A love so passionate as theirs would have predictably burned itself out very quickly. What Maeztu does not seem to be aware of as well is that in order for fictional love to be memorable it has to be truncated by death.[11] From Greek mythology, Dante and Beatrice, Romeo and Juliet to Don Juan and Doña Inés, death has doomed and simultaneously immortalized the great romances of time. Suffering, not the satisfaction of love, is what stirs us.[12]

Though Celestina's intervention results in Calisto's first tryst with Melibea, the price the lovers pay is high indeed. Celestina's profound knowledge of human nature, not her demonic machinations, make her a character so powerful that she nearly becomes the primary moving force of the play. Overcoming obstacle after obstacle, she deftly turns Melibea's resistance into eagerness and then proceeds to enlist the help of Calisto's servants for her campaign to fleece the impatient and rich lover. Sempronio's greed easily put him on her side; Pármeno is another matter. The method she employs to ascertain his weakness, a need that were she to satisfy it, would give her an upper hand in her dealings with Calisto, closely follows the pattern established earlier in Melibea's downfall. She ferrets out his secret by probing his desires as a man—money, faithfulness, and finally love, his lust for Areusa. A prostitute of Celestina's, this girl becomes the decoy through which the old woman entraps the recalcitrant Pármeno. Her tasks admirably accomplished, all that remains is reaping the rewards of her success. Celestina's death occurs when she unaccountably refuses to share her payment with Pármeno and Sempronio. How can this fatal mistake by the wise, calculating Celestina, in denying the covetous Sempronio his share, be explained? Maeztu, like many before and after him, does not know what to answer. Perhaps Celestina allows greed to get the best of her, feeling that neither did enough to warrant their sharing in the gold necklace, a difficult item to divide among three; or else at sixty years of age she is thinking of the days when she may no longer be able to practice her arts. Being human she cannot escape error, which costs her her life. This failing, however, does not detract from her pragmatic wisdom; for Maeztu she is its literary personalification.

Celestina is pleasure's high priestess. Her profession as procuress repels those who pride themselves on moral rectitude, yet she is not easy to dismiss. Not only does she ply her trade successfully, but she also argues its benefits very convincingly. Maeztu calls Celestina hedonism's saint, because for her there is no god other than pleasure. Indeed, her whole life is dedicated to providing that commodity, in her youth by giving her body, and in old age by trafficking with other women's. Considering it as nothing more than running a business like any other, she claims that she beats at no doors soliciting; on the contrary, many—including priests and other dignitaries—knock on hers seeking her services. Celestina only looks to satisfy men's pleasures at a profit for herself. Her fault may be that she does not believe in pleasures other than those of the flesh (she herself is an alcoholic). At this juncture Maeztu himself pronounces his skepticism of Stuart Mill (philosophy's modern hedonist) and his contention that art, reason, and social service make up superior pleasures. Government subsidization of museums, schools, and social programs contrasts sharply with the huge taxes levied on alcoholic beverages or the persecution to which prostitution is subject everywhere. The verdict is unmistakably clear when the former have to be artificially supported to make them viable, while the latter have to be curbed constantly so as to check their spread. Human nature, that side of it representing man devoid of honor and morality, manifests itself through Celestina. Her argument, irrefutable from a utilitarian point of view, becomes repugnant only because goodness can be distinguished from pleasure and because, in Maeztu's belief, in society man's moral half has prevailed. Celestina stands for man against society, the momentous satisfaction of sensual vice against the reason required for survival into the future.

The clear division of *La Celestina's* characters into the go-between's apologists and her detractors leads Maeztu to consider its author as a man moved by a deeply troubled soul. He is of the opinion that Fernando de Rojas probably was an apostate Jew who professed a newly adopted Catholicism just so he could remain in Spain. The religious-moral aspect of the authorship interests Maeztu far more than the civil identity of the person or persons who put together the three basic versions of *La Celestina* (Burgos 1499, 16 acts; Seville 1502, 21 acts; Toledo 1526, 22 acts).

The Catholic Kings, Ferdinand and Isabella, issued a decree of expulsion of all the Jews from Spanish territories in 1492. The exiles had, aside from official alternatives of abjuring Judaism and converting to Catholicism or leaving the country, the option of staying and feigning conversion, secretly worshipping Jehovah. The case of Fernando de Rojas reveals yet a fourth attitude in Maeztu's view, one perhaps not exclusive to our author. There seems little doubt that for expediency's sake Rojas chose to renounce his faith and to embrace Catholicism, but Maeztu suspects that Rojas was equally disinterested in both religions. The teachings of two religions that share the Ten Commandments and portray a world guided by a just God where virtue is rewarded was something which as a youth Rojas might have believed, but no longer. The man who wrote *La Celestina* was a skeptic who saw life in different terms. For him neither justice nor morality rule this earth; life commonly does not make sense; greed and passion as often as not win out. Without a god to provide an order of things, chance, war, and other blind forces are entrusted with man's destiny. The microcosm portrayed in *La Celestina* shows a score of people overtaken by blind passions which drive them to their own destruction. Its ultimate message, then, notwithstanding the moral bits and pieces sprinkled here and there, together with its avowed didactic nature (which served to shield work and author from the fires of the Inquisition), amounts to a bitter indictment of life. In *La Celestina*, as in Don Juan, Maeztu finds that Spaniards are presented with the possibility of life without ideals.

Basically what convinces Maeztu of Rojas' Jewish ascendancy are the two catalysts in the play, carnal desire and greed. This bares an anti-Semitic prejudice shared by other members of the Generation of 1898, Baroja above all. In Maeztu's defense, however, it can be stated that no malicious intent accompanied his authorial detective work; rather than religious or racial, it can better be classified as an anthropological characterization reaching no further than many commonplace notions of what typifies an individual of Jewish background. Rojas, befitting a spirit indifferent to both Judaism and Roman Catholicism, neither condones greed nor condemns lust in absolute terms. The former religion traditionally encourages the accumulation of material wealth as being compatible with moral rectitude, but severely condemns sexual transgressions. The latter faith, on the other hand, considers wealth an impediment to salvation and looks more forgivingly upon sins of lust.

As a youth, Rojas learned that piety, resourcefulness, wealth, knowledge, and honor were supreme virtues. His character Celestina personifies wisdom and dialectic subtlety and she is rich too, but all of these attributes she possesses in a perverted manner—a hedonist priestess symbolizing the demythologizing of the rabbinical ideal. Similarly Calisto and Melibea, noble, wealthy, honorable, and generous, forsake the rational mentality preached in the *Talmud* and choose to lose themselves in a passionate love whatever the risk. In both cases, virtue paves the way for evil and destruction in an inversion of "Israel's table of values" (160). *La Celestina* is no Catholic manifesto either. The use of suicide as a personal choice of action, or the accusations levelled against the clergy, make every critic ponder how the work ever eluded the Inquisition.

Rojas discerns no appreciable goal in life and therefore questions the validity of sacrifice on the part of man. Such, declares Maeztu, is the attitude of the religious skeptic. This vein of incredulousness is found in Spaniards throughout the centuries where it originated, according to him, precisely with Jews like Rojas, and Arabs who, when forced to give up their own religion, did not wholeheartedly accept the new dogmas imposed on them. Too many times Spaniards have given up an undertaking, heeding those who, like Rojas, disillusioned, underestimate life's values, or who look upon death as the great destroyer, and even those who, on the other hand, aim so low in their materialistic pursuits that no moral individual could ever be satisfied with their set goal. Maeztu's answer is to look upon the business of this world in light of the next, to operate here in the larger context of what lies beyond the threshold of death. He proposes that to instill greater sense into life, man needs to live in terms of an everlasting existence.

The measure of this world lies in the next. And so when the spectacle of evil triumphant continues to alternate irrationally with virtue recompensed, its perception need not dismay man. Viewed in the wider perspective of a moral universe, the individual may not always receive justice, but a society will be given justice. Quoting Hegel's phrase "world history is the world's supreme court" (168), Maeztu insists that it is the individual who needs and must believe in the afterlife. Maeztu sees in life, even as portrayed in *La Celestina,* an unaccountable degree of chance, suggestive of an unresolved moral dilemma and representing an imbalance of virtue and reward.

Egotistic knowledge devoid of all other positive qualities leads nowhere. As with Don Quijote's love or Don Juan's power, Celestina's wisdom is misdirected, but not irretrievably so, as with them. In his discursive commentary, Maeztu has demonstrated the formidable potential of each of these three attributes in function of the others. Their essential nature as myths, incarnated in these figures of literature, would not prevent them from being appropriated by Spaniards of his time. "A legend," he thought, "is more real than history." Operating with the cautions suggested throughout the essays, Maeztu wanted Spain to believe in the efficacy of these three values as strongly as he did, because by heeding them the nation would achieve a greater place in the world.

CHAPTER 6

The Counterrevolutionary Doctrine

RAMIRO de Maeztu arrived in Buenos Aires on February 21, 1928, as Spain's Ambassador to Argentina. While he remained in that capacity until 1930, Maeztu actively participated in the capital city's literary life, giving speeches or appearing at cultural functions. Few critics today doubt that it was then that he conceived and began the early elaboration of his main work *Defensa de la Hispanidad* (*In Defense of Hispanism*) published in 1934 in Madrid, a few years after his definitive return to Spain. On May 11, 1929, Maeztu delivered a lecture on "El sentido del hombre en los pueblos hispánicos" ("The Meaning of Man in Spanish Countries") at the Gallegan cultural center in Montevideo. It is the first version of the book's second chapter, "El valor de la hispanidad" ("The Worth of Hispanism"), which was originally to have served as the title of the book instead of *In Defense of Hispanism*.

Maeztu is usually remembered for this doctrinal treatise, inevitably characterized as its archreactionary author. The advocates of *In Defense of Hispanism*, who are few, consider it one of the most important books of Spanish counterrevolutionary thought and the theoretical basis of a whole perspective of Franco's foreign policy for the years immediately following the country's civil war.[1] There is no doubt as to its vogue at that time. In less than ten years the book had gone through more than twenty editions.[2] Its point of view contrasts with the negative attitude of the Generation of 1898,[3] even with Maeztu's own earlier stance as a passive and disillusioned critic. What earlier had been renounced by them all, Maeztu now embraces as the only possible salvation, the return to the traditional ideals which had carried Spain to her greatest glory in history, the time of the

114

conquest and civilization of America. These ideals were country, faith, language, and culture. [4]

This work also marks another departure. Whereas in his youth Maeztu had focused his attention on Spain, now, in *In Defense of Hispanism*, he takes in a much more ambitious panorama. [5] All of the Spanish-speaking world is now the scenario for Maeztu's passionate and polemic defense of a historical messianism which, being uniquely native to Spain, he called "Hispanidad" (Hispanism).

I *Hispanism and Its Diffusion*

In the spirit of the terms *Cristianidad* ("Christianity"), designating a host of nations of the same religious creed, and *Humanidad* ("Humanity"), meaning all mankind, Maeztu coined the word *Hispanidad* ("Hispanism") to characterize the brotherhood of Hispanic countries. His criteria were neither geographic nor anthropological, but cultural and political in purpose. [6] He saw as members of this community those nations which, dating back to 1492, owe their language, religion, values, and ideals to a mother country, Spain. At times the unity of this family of nations may appear shaky, especially when the two historical bases which engendered it, Catholicism and a monarchical regime, are cast aside. Nevertheless efforts to deny a common heritage do not preclude the possibility of a present-day alliance in Maeztu's design.

Though weakened, the spirit of Hispanism subsists. The crisis that ultimately led to the separation of Spain from her colonies began in the mother country itself. For Maeztu the catalyst was the "Encyclopedia" and the French Revolution. The colonies were lost, in theory, in the middle of the eighteenth century. It was at that point when Spain, marvelling at the business prowess of Great Britain and the Low Countries, and at the luxury of Versailles, ashamed of her poverty, forsook the ideals she had defended, believing that all that was foreign was best. Spain opened her doors to the cultural and spiritual dominance of France in particular. Some good came of it such as the founding of academies of higher learning, construction of new roads and canals, building of museums, revamping of an archaic economic structure, and a revision of disciplines of study at all levels. However, as advantageous as this updating may have been, the fact remains that when the country stopped following the course previously chartered, a change of spirit ensued. At the time no one saw that a change of ideals implied a discontinuance with tradition that would lead to the dissolution of the empire and a distancing from the colonies. But from the moment Spain's regime included a pragmatic ordering in the economic, military, and territorial spheres, the bonds of fealty were broken—the viceroys of the New World easily perceived that the country in whose name they governed during the second half of the eighteenth century no longer stood for the same evangelical purpose decreed in the testament of Queen Isabella: "Her principal end and intention, and that of the King, her consort, in pacifying and populating the West Indies, was to convert to the Holy Catholic Faith the natives" (46).[7]

What Maeztu, the society "Acción Española," and its journal of the same name propose is embracing those values that had been the keystone of Spain's tradition for centuries but that had been given up two hundred years back. He no longer demands the Europeanizing of his country, but places the greatness of Spain in a faithfulness to its traditions. His hopes for a reversal of the trend away from traditional values are fed by isolated cries of protest throughout Spanish America. These voices, still in a minority and not quite fully convinced that Hispanism's moral principles of the sixteenth and seventeenth centuries were vastly superior to those of the countries emulated and compatible with their drive for independence, show an awareness that Spain's ideal must not have been "entirely despicable if they provided three centuries of peace and progress" (54).

Hispanism created world history, asserts Maeztu, by discovering the sea routes connecting the Orient with the West, thereby geographically constituting it into a unit. And secondly, by ensuring that at the Council of Trent the dogma which guarantees every man the possibility of salvation prevailed, Spain elevated humanity to a common spiritual level. By virtue of these two feats Spain accomplished what no nation had achieved up to that time or has since then. Reflecting upon the system of beliefs, laws, morals, and sentiments which enabled Spain to carry out her mission, they do not seem to pale in comparison with those of other countries which she envied, to her disadvantage. Just the opposite, says Maeztu; in spite of the shortcomings already noted in sixteenth- to seventeenth-century Spain, on the whole she was on the right track and pointed the way to a certain future. Further evidence derives from the discredit of Rousseau, the utopian system of Marx and Engels, and the unworkable practices of liberal democracies.

Spain lost her Golden Age ideal and subsequently fell into decline; she fell under France's complete dominance in the course of the eighteenth century. Those are historical facts. On the other hand, to assert that had she dismissed these influences, the course of her history would have continued on the path of greatness is something else. Could she have resisted such influence even if she had wanted to? Maeztu does not adhere to historical data. He has an axe to grind, and philosophizes about history. Monarchy and religion are the keys to his historical projections. If we accept these premises as he sees them, then the development of his thesis, if not entirely convincing, is at least easily discernible.

Maeztu's historical philosophy is an adaptation of his German professor Nicolai Hartmann's structure of history doused with a generous portion of Catholic providentialism.[8] Hartmann perceived history as the integration of four superimposed layers: matter (geography), the lowest; life, supported by matter, but with its own laws, follows; above them lies the soul, autonomous as well; and finally at the highest level we find the objective spirit (i.e., God) possessing its own laws and freedom.[9] Maeztu inserts into this text the "Dogma of Sufficient Grace" defended by Spanish theologians (Diego Laínez, S.J.) at Trent; there is sufficient grace to enable every man to save his soul merely through a "will to salvation," in other words, through his own efforts. From this dogma derives the missionary idea that Maeztu thought was Spain's destiny in the world; to carry to all men the divine finality of life and its intrinsically salvationist nature.[10]

II   *The Worth of Hispanism*

Another figure of the Generation of 1898, Angel Ganivet, had written in his best known work, *Idearium Español (Spanish Ideologue)* published in 1897, that Spain's innermost core was made up of an indestructible moral fiber which guarded her men both in victory and defeat. The nature of that precious matter, he felt, derived from Seneca's Stoicism. According to Ganivet, Stoicism, while protecting men in times of adversity, has made Spaniards aware that truth resides in no particular nation, and that victory does not signal an intrinsic superiority on the part of the victor over the vanquished. Yet, Maeztu adds, most Spaniards also yearn for a permanence of things which are doomed to temporal extinction such as friendship, love, and pleasure. This weakness turns the impassive attitude of the few true Stoics into what Maeztu labels "Spanish humanism" (66). Based on the Catholic dogma stressing equality among men,

"Spanish humanism" is a truer "diamond-hard" axis of Spanish peoples' lives for Maeztu than Ganivet's idealistic Stoicism.

The root of modern humanism stems from Protagoras' contention that man is the measure of all things. Truth and goodness exist only in relation to man. Truth is what man feels is believable and completely satisfying to him; goodness, what man considers beneficial and pleasing to him. Thus, "Humanism and Relativism," concludes Maeztu, "are synonymous" (69). Revitalized by the Renaissance this form of secular humanism continued to dominate in the world that Maeztu appraised in the early nineteen-hundreds. Everywhere, that is, except in Spain. Neither secular or, as he called it, "materialistic humanism" nor "arrogant humanism" ever made deep inroads into Spain.

The humanism of arrogance drives those who consider themselves superior to other faiths, races, or nations. "Materialistic humanism," a contradiction which Maeztu doesn't seem to mind so long as he can catalog it next to other perversions of this multifaceted philosophy, devalues truth and goodness, proclaiming their lack of significance. This type of humanism (communism in Maeztu's terms), declares equality among men emphasizing a corporeal equality while negating the existence of a soul, a denial that foreshadows its ultimate failure, for Maeztu considers patently false the assertion that men are corporally equal, that they have the same skills, inclinations, or characters, or that they will work for the common good without individual rewards or recognition.

Between these two attitudes, the exclusiveness of arrogance and the levelling of sameness, lies the Spanish position. To Maeztu's mind it was Don Quijote who first formulated his country's sense of humanism when he said to Sancho Panza: "No one is better than anybody else if he doesn't do more than anybody else" (78). Socially speaking, there exist many strata revealing hierarchical categories, but within those differing levels (e. g., a duke and a cook) it is possible that the duke could be a scoundrel and the cook a righteous man. Essentially both men are equal so that a choice within their station exists. Sancho compares all men to chess pieces, when on the board they represent differing degrees of power, but once the game is done all go into the same box (81).

Such an indulgent attitude accounts for the lenient sentences in Spain's justice system which many would claim stems from her Catholic beliefs but, says Maeztu, Spanish nonbelievers are of the same persuasion as those who practice their religion. In a historical context, Spain has always been persuaded of a spiritual equality among men. Spaniards did not try to pass themselves off as superior beings when they could have done so easily at the time of the colonization of the New World. Admittedly many inexcusable abuses were perpetrated against the Indians, but the legislation specifically created for governing the colonies remains without par in the safeguards provided for the new subjects. "We Spaniards have never considered ourselves a superior people. . . . What we have thought to be superior is our credo of the essential equality among men" (83). The supreme power enjoyed by Spain in the sixteenth and seventeenth centuries never gave rise to a feeling of arrogance, as happened in the case of the Arabs in the eighth century, even if her men knew they were fighting God's battles. Religious nationalism had not been, nor was it at the time of Maeztu's writing, characteristic of Spain's history, a factor which he felt sure contributed directly to the country's downhill slide of the past two hundred years.

Ironically, the country's ecumenical stance explains also, in part, some of Spain's flaws. Spaniards, having never felt superior, began to believe those who considered them to be inferior. Such was the state of mind which paved the way for her decline as a world power. The quintessence of Spain's Golden Age was defined as "the possibility of salvation of all men on earth" (87) by Maeztu. That proclamation amounted to the cornerstone of human progress and the greatest treasure harbored by all Hispanic peoples as far as he was concerned; insuring its communication to the widest number of men remained the charge of Spain's people. To demonstrate its value, however, Spain must prove it with deeds that others can see and judge.

The Stoics believed that all men were children of the same God, a parentage that did not exclude for them an intellectual aristocracy where the wise (the Stoics themselves) acted in accord with inner strength while the rest of men were moved by circumstance. It was perfectly possible for a slave, like Epictetus, to belong to this segregated elite insofar as he could resist the embattlement of circumstance and remain unmoved. What distinguished the Stoics from the Catholics, declares Maeztu, is that the former felt that only God could induce men to behave wisely, whereas the latter can do so of their own free will and effort.

If Spaniards at one time in their history deviated from their belief in equality, when in the sixteenth and seventeenth centuries certificates of "cleanliness of blood" (that one was an "old Christian" and not a "new" or recently converted one) were demanded of those who sought high or important charges, it was not for racial or even for religious reasons but because a country at war with heretics and infidels needed to ascertain the true commitment of its agents.

Ganivet's "diamond-hard axis" does not contradict the principles of liberty, equality, and brotherhood, so dear to every rebel's heart since the French Revolution; it includes them all and yet Spain has never appropriated them for herself. Morally, Spaniards maintain the principle of liberty because for them man, no matter how grievous his sins, can always repent, or elect never to do so. But a man cannot be considered good or bad unless he enjoys the freedom of choice to act wisely or wrongly. Political liberty derives from the recognition of this moral liberty to act, man cannot do good unless he acts freely. But here Maeztu contends that man, corruptor of nature and in turn corrupted by her, must live in a society organized so as to deter his capacity for evil and to excite his will to work constructively. This is a continuance of Maeztu's apologue for a coercive government, based on the reward-punishment ethic latent in Roman Catholicism. He grudgingly recognizes the validity of Stuart Mills' celebrated sentence, "If all mankind minus one were of one opinion, and only one person were of the contrary opinion, mankind would be no more justified in silencing that one person, than he, if he had the power, would be justified in silencing mankind" (98). Maeztu realizes that had Christ or Socrates been silenced at the outset of their adult lives, the world would have been much the worse for it.

The greatest living British liberal philosopher of Maeztu's day was, of course, Bertrand Russell, and Maeztu rails against him time and again, especially attacking Russell's "Principle of Growth." Its theory was that man instinctively proceeded in the direction which best suited him; therefore he had to be allowed the freedom to follow his impulses, for denial would produce an awakening of man's worst instincts. Maeztu sees in this nothing more than a rehash of Rousseau's "noble savage" disproved by two hundred years of failures in Romanticism. The politician Donoso Cortés' words that low political repression corresponds to high religious fervor, and high political repression and instability correspond to a low religious temperature are taken as gospel by Maeztu. Sociopolitical well-being demands that individual drives be directed, and if necessary coerced to the common good. In this context religion provides guidance as to the nature of good and evil through the example of crime and punishment.

The most misguided of men may one day realize his mistake and mend his ways. In this capacity to recognize error and ultimately achieve salvation lies the true equality among men; no one is so high that he can't fall or so low that he can't raise himself. But, aside from this common ability to convert, or spiritual equality, there exists no other equality for Maeztu. Some men are intelligent, others slow-thinking, some strong, others weak, and so on. When two leaves coming from the same tree are not the same, how can any two men be alike? asks Maeztu. As for the concept of brotherhood among men, what other basis can it have, save for the consciousness that God is the Father of all men? A familial relationship is already established by the fact that they can all be saved or condemned according to their actions on this earth.

Individual interests must be deferred on behalf of the community, a sacrifice that religion can sanction. This is one of religion's principal functions according to Maeztu, accounting for the success of Spaniards of the Golden Age; then men were persuaded they fought, lived, and died for God's greater glory. Nothing else distinguished Spain of the sixteenth and seventeenth centuries, in Maeztu's opinion, from the Spain of the twentieth century. In fact he saw the old Spain as poorer, less populated, and less educated than in his time. Consequently he felt that all that was needed was to reestablish the social climate propitious to man's willing betterment of himself. The question that remains explicitly unanswered is: How? By the combined power of the State and the Church as it had been three hundred years earlier, Maeztu seems to be suggesting. An unrealistic goal since Spain, in spite of her isolation from Europe and subsequently the New World, does not function in a vacuum, unaffected by the rest of the nations.

In his own mind Maeztu believes that Spain's accomplishments have no peer in world history. To have carried civilization to the New World where human sacrifice, incest, slavery, and cannibalism prevailed was an enormous feat, for it meant uprooting customs dating back hundreds of years, but more momentous than this was to have instilled in those people a consciousness of the moral unity in all mankind, not only among themselves but with the newcomers, their conquerors and teachers. The greater credit for this labor goes to the religious orders that, beginning in 1510, not only taught the existence and meaning of one God but restrained the excesses and rapacity of the viceroys and the *encomenderos*.

Normally missionaries went along with soldiers on military expeditions to help settle and indoctrinate the new territories. Starting with the reign of Charles V, no action could begin without prior consent of these priests. There existed a unique compenetration of temporal and spiritual powers. Soldier and missionary acted in full accord, each fighting for an ideal which corresponded with the other's. It was a theocratic state, for Maeztu Spain's greatest hour, which he hopes will again inspire not only his own country but the rest of the world as well. The assimilation of races carried out by Spain through the cross and the sword should be taken as a lesson, not just as some past history but as a guide to integrate all of the world's races. This is the reason why the years (1545–1563) of the Council of Trent represent for Maeztu the peak of Spain's spiritual hegemony in history.

Spain, her soldiers, priests, and common people, all acted as missionaries in the sixteenth and seventeenth centuries. "Santa Teresa speaks like a soldier" (125), writes Maeztu, implying that religion was something that had to be "defended," "protected," and, more importantly, "imparted." The Society of Jesus had at its helm not a director but a general. Its founder, Ignatius of Loyola, considered the spread of Catholicism so essential to Spain's victory in the New World that he sent his best-loved lieutenant, Francis Xavier, whom Jesuits regarded as Loyola's alter ego. This total dedication on the part of every Spaniard to proselytize overseas led to a drain of energy and resources in the country rendering it defenseless against the "fascination exerted by foreign civilization" (127). More than a few Jesuit, Dominican, and Franciscan friars died at the hands of the Indians, but by the time the Jesuits were expelled from South America and their order later dissolved, the former savages were left with an indelible mark which kept them from regressing into their tribal customs. Their racial origin notwithstanding, many would rule equally with Spaniards over their own countries because of the doctrine instilled in them that on a spiritual level their equality with all other men was beyond question. In such a process Maeztu saw the basic distinction which separated Spain from other colonial powers such as Great Britain. The Philippines, under Spain's control until 1898, demonstrated how the conqueror shared her language, religion, customs, and government with the conquered. India, on the other hand, offered an example of a dominated people constantly reminded, by aristocratic English elitism of the most blatant segregationist nature, of their lot as the vanquished, sharing nothing with their colonizers except perhaps a mutual disdain for one another.

In Maeztu's time and before there were Spanish missionaries in

China, in the jungles of the Amazon, and in central Africa as well. Their duty ended in South America, they dispersed over the globe, a move Maeztu considers invaluable for the struggle against communism, but that, by itself, is largely ineffectual. The Church on its own cannot overcome the overwhelming power of a huge nation bent on spreading its influence. Needed for such a struggle is a union of Church and State similar to that in Spain's sixteenth and seventeenth centuries to ensure that the hammer and sickle do not some day prevail over the sign of the cross. Maeztu thinks that "intermediate solutions are less probable each day" (138). For him it was not enough to resist communism; it had to be crushed since it represented not only a political and social system but a kind of perverted religion in its denial of man's spiritual or moral dimension.

III *Hispanism's Crisis*

The relationship between the United States and England, competition with each other but solidarity before the world, characterizes the ideal link between two countries, except that such a model cannot be emulated by Spain and her former colonies since it is based on the belief of Anglo-Saxon hegemony and, for Maeztu, this means a racial distinction heretofore unpracticed by Spaniards. His reason for singling out this international relationship is that race does not necessarily constitute the only basis for an alliance. True, Spain never considered her men a superior race, but she did believe at one time in the superiority of her Catholic ideal. National independence and geographical dispersion notwithstanding, this superior ideal could have had the same linking effect among the Hispanic nations. But the solidarity was lost when the ideal was forgotten and each nation not only went her own way, but at times even fought with the others.

When experiments to pattern their governments in the style of eighteenth-century France failed, the blame did not fall on Rousseau or Montesquieu but on Spain's earlier lessons. The culprit was Spain, for having introduced in its own bureaucracy the ideals of the Enlightenment and then exporting them to the New World where they slowly undermined the bonds between the mother country and her colonies. Their common ideal, forged upon the belief in an Almighty God, waned before dazzling French revolutionary notions. The Indians for a period turned their backs on their new God and the *criollos* (children of Spaniards born in the New World) forsook work for political intrigue on behalf of something called independence. Simón Bolívar, the "great liberator," grew up in the

new cultural ambient fostered by Spaniards themselves who sought
to please France and other European nations more "advanced" than
they felt Spain was at that time. The Spanish monarchs, beginning
with Charles II, believed that one way of preserving the empire was
to become France's ally, and they flattered France, copying her
manners, her styles, and her ideals. Spain became an echo of her
neighbor to the north, her writers became translators or imitators,
her noble classes dressed in French styles and spoke French. Spain
betrayed herself thinking what France wanted her to think (165).

In railing against France, Maeztu singles out Rousseau's
naturalism, the theory of the noble savage, as the most noxious
influence. Intellectually it does not appear to him as a formidable
philosophical edifice, but as a human tendency, naturalism "is almost
irresistible" (167). Religiously, morally, and politically this doctrine
unravels all of civilizations's accomplishments, a challenge that
Spain, in a Europeanizing phase, was not strong enough to counter.
In the New World particularly, the effect was disastrous on the
Indians and perplexing for the *criollos*. Discipline was relaxed,
culture became in some ways suspect, and politics edged toward the
will of the majority.

While in the past a few isolated voices in South America had been
Spain's apologists, beginning in 1898 with Rubén Darío, the number
of authors who began to write on behalf of the founding country
gradually increased to a significant figure. Ironically, Darío's reputation rested not only on the worth of his verses but on the anti-Spanish
nature of all his work. A confirmed Francophile, he went to Spain
following the 1898 fiasco as a correspondent for the Buenos Aires
daily *La Nación* to appraise the situation of the defeated. Instead, he
remained there until his death, writing some of his best poetry, much
of it in praise of Spain as a defender of Hispanism. Many others
followed—Enrique Larreta, Manuel Gálvez, Joaquín Edwards Bello,
Reyles, Vallenilla Lanz, Arturo Capdevila. Rubén Darío represents
for Maeztu the first truly Spanish-American individual who happens
to be a poet, but more importantly a universal man who casts his eyes
on Spain and recognizes the worth of her values, and the urgency of
pursuing the concept of Hispanism, capable of uniting them all once
again. The flaw lies in the fact that, had Spanish America looked to
Spain earlier, it would have found Spain wanting, unsure of herself
and thus unable to provide a steady spiritual leadership on which to
rebuild a Hispanic alliance.

The vacuum as a result of Spain's exit from the New World in 1898 was progressively filled with two rival powers equally opposed to the spirit of Hispanism, the United States and Russia. But neither the U.S. dollar diplomacy nor the Soviet revolutionary tactics made deep impressions on the character of life in South America. Both failed to a degree because capitalist policies on the one hand were short sighted and, on the other, Russia's export-type revolution needed more time to germinate discontent among a wider social swath. And, as Maeztu had written earlier, a certain neutralizing effect resulted from the struggle for power that these two nations waged at a distance. Consequently the vacuum remained, one that Maeztu believes can only be filled by a positive spiritual force.

After World War I Maeztu looked around and envied no country. Plagued by huge deficits, war debts, and ruined industries the defeated nations lay with the victors, crippled by unemployment due to the progress of technology and mechanization. Their ideals led these nations to destruction and inflation of terrifying proportions. No nation Spanish-American leaders had admired or feared is excepted, France, Germany, Italy, or the United States. These "gods" gone, Maeztu seems to be saying, there remains only the return to Spain and the true God at the center of her ideals. Taking stock of themselves, Spanish-American countries will realize that the norm they seek for the future can be found in their own past. Their future is secure only insofar as they acknowledge that their most important mission continues to be the messianic task of incorporating all nonbelievers to the ranks of Catholicism. Paradoxically then, writes Maeztu, the future of a nation very much hinges on its fidelity to its past. He is referring to the essential past which coexists with an individual or a nation because it is part of its character.

Maeztu considers it folly to try and gain strength by change that will do away with significant fundamental attributes of a country. He himself, in his early *Toward a New Spain,* had sought a stronger nation but devoid of her traditions and cultural values, a goal he now recognized as impossible. Whenever an object pretends to acquire attributes extraneous to its own, it will cease being essentially what it originally was. In order to gain strength, the Spanish-American countries must "re-enforce their own being" (193), which still bears the imprint of sixteenth- and seventeenth-century Spain. For Maeztu, their mission remains ever important. The West needs strengthening in its religious underpinnings, the East is yet to be won over to Catholicism. Hispanism's burden perhaps need no longer be borne solely by the family of Spanish nations. World War I over, the novelty of modern values had worn off and many countries might look Spain's way and, if she were wise, follow her in the establishment of a spiritual universality based on Catholic values.

Just as Rubén Darío and other Spanish Americans had reevaluated their attitudes toward Spain beginning in 1898, Maeztu notes that the rest of the world begins at the turn of the century to praise Spanish historical ideals. Her relationship with the Arabs and the Jews, institutions such as the earlier defamed Inquisition, Phillip II and his policies, all are reexamined and placed in a more equitable light, acceptable from Spain's own vantage point. The vindication comes as a result of history's pendular movement. Spain's weakened position at the time facilitated these concessions from nations secure in their first rank positions. Then too, the era being reevaluated, Spain's Golden Age, represented an ordered world where cause and effect could easily be determined, and when events could be controlled to one's advantage. Contrasted with a world dominated by forces uncontrollable by any one nation, Spain's period of hegemony held understandable appeal. For Maeztu, however, looking back two centuries was no wishful dream. He firmly believed that those years constituted a program to be followed, guidelines which could be implemented if the will to do it existed—the need was obviously there.

In Maeztu's opinion, Spanish character was determined largely by two historical struggles, one against the Arabs, the other against the Jews. In the eighth-century campaign to resist Arabic religious fatalism, Spain acquired a firm conviction that man can be master of his own destiny. From the fight against the exclusiveness that characterizes Judaism, Spaniards resolved that no race is privileged, that any man is as good as the next. These two principles, freedom of choice for each man and equality among men, that Spain sought to propagate throughout her new territories have not maintained her hegemony in the world because they were traded away for the unproven, fatuous, and ultimately mistaken policies of France and England in the 1700's. Nevertheless, if Spain was the first to experience a decline, the apologists of such doctrines did not lag too far behind. For Maeztu the inescapable conclusion is that Spain's deviation from her original ideals being proven erroneous, the nation would now have enough confidence to chart her own course.

As Maeztu interpreted the international scene in the early twenties and thirties, the greatest danger to a new Hispanic league did not stem from undue foreign influence. Those nations which earlier had posed such a threat, France and England, and subsequently the

United States and Russia, now had socioeconomic troubles of their own so that the prestige with which they had managed to fascinate Spain and Spanish America was all but gone. Instead, the crisis which might likely plague them would now come from within, though its seeds had been imported mainly from France—naturalism. Maeztu viewed it as a "radical negation of all spiritual values" (216), compatible with the other democratic notion which stipulates economic equality for everyone. He had no use for democracy which he saw as a government doomed to failure for its practice of dispensing patronage jobs which would fatten the State's payroll to the point of bankruptcy. The devaluation of post-World War I marks, pounds, and francs sufficed to convince him. What Maeztu proposes instead is a State where government employment does not automatically open the way for personal and party gain. Officials, finding employment in the private sector more remunerative, would serve their country aware that their reward for excelling in so doing would only come in the form of self-satisfaction and public acknowledgment. The "Booty-State," as he calls it, is the political expression of a naturalist sense of life. The "Service-State" (his own) is inspired by a moral or religious sense of life.

Hispanism's crisis, then, reverts to a question of religious principles, beginning when Spain's most influential State leaders no longer believed that the principles of its government had to be one with its Catholic religion. The secularization began in the look to the outside world, followed by a loss of self-confidence, and ultimately by the loss of religious faith. By the beginning of the twentieth century, however, the tide had turned in Spain's favor: her historical role was being vindicated abroad as well as at home; Catholicism was once again on the upswing. Those countries once hostile to Spain were now undergoing crises of their own, and democracies were found to be too expensive. Maeztu may have been right, but he was too optimistic. He set up straw men for the sole purpose of knocking them down, ingenuously leaving only one "solution" at the end—the establishment of a government founded on altruistic service by a morally educated elite which would gradually school the masses with their example. Such a State would then spontaneously foster a strong Hispánic alliance among all the Spanish countries (223).

IV *The Essence of Hispanism*

Before Maeztu can formulate his definitive advocacy of Hispanism, it becomes necessary for him to explain why the twenty-odd nations to make up such an alliance often behaved as though no common bond existed. The beginning of international brotherhood lies in the concept of country, in a patriotic sense, an ideal Maeztu considers sacred in every sense of the term. Canovas' sentence, "One stands by one's Country right or wrong, just as one stands by one's father and mother" (229), and Maura's motto, "One does not choose one's Country" (229), represent basically Maeztu's thought.

"Territory, race and cultural values" nurture a citizen's patriotism, though not with equal fervor, and certainly in varying degrees. Catalonians feel strongest about territorial rights; Basques put racial pride above all else. From this heterogeneity, Maeztu feels, stem the problems of national unity and of the larger union which is Hispanism. He understands the essence of the patriotic notion to be spiritual. Consequently Spain, as a country, has its inception in the year 586 when the Visigoth King Recaredo converted to Catholicism and declared his religion the State's official one. The moment law and faith become one for the first time, Spain acquires the three preestablished essentials for nationhood: race, territory, and unifying cultural values (i.e., religious or spiritual values). The 12th of October, 1492, marks symbolically the birth of Hispanism since the founding of empire had at its core a spiritual purpose, to spread among the heathen a religion that preached equality for all men. Religion sustained Spain in spite of international injustices for over two centuries. The foundation of a country, for Maeztu, must be a superior value or set of values. The value which gave birth to Spain was Recaredo's abjuration of Arianism and his conversion to Catholicism. The individual must dedicate himself to a superior value since to do so will insure the prosperity of his country.

Maeztu's assumption that a nation's values are generally laudable explains why he agrees with Canovas' and Maura's unequivocal pledges of allegiance. He further assumes that the moral value of an ideal constitutes a desirable or pragmatic national goal and equates moral idealism with practical reality (a reproach he himself makes of others). The *ab initio* obedience of the governed to the governors that he proposes suggests a willing authoritarianism. The basis is clear since Canovas' statement equates civil with divine law (obedience to one's government should emulate obedience owed to one's parents). To justify such a blind trust, Maeztu reaches for the often-heard notion that those at the helm know best because they know more. He conceives patriotism as a spiritual entity upon which the territorial and racial future and worth of a nation rest, but which supersedes them both. The quotation from Saint Augustine's *De libero arbitrio*,

"Always love your fellowmen, and more than your fellowmen, your parents, and more than your parents, your country, and more than your country, love God" (253), attests to his continuing belief that only through Catholic moral principles can a country endure.

Tradition is the best school from which to learn. It will serve to help Spaniards discern where and when they strayed from the correct way in history. The country had always looked up to those men who worked for the public interest rather than those who sought to do themselves the most good while in high office. From the earliest and humblest of her leaders, beginning with the guerrilla leader Viriato, in the time of the Romans, Spain has preferred those who put the country's welfare above their own, an example not to be dismissed. In the realm of jurisprudence, Spain for many centuries meted out justice with admirable equanimity. The machinery, based on a moral code upheld equally throughout the kingdom and supported by the throne, provided a system of justice unequaled in modern times. The change for the worse dates from the eighteenth century, when justice meant the application of a code of laws derived not from moral principles but from the sovereign, collective or individual. The letter of the law became more important than its spirit. Divorced from the principle that laws needed to be just and moral, Maeztu points to the tragic abandonment of tradition as guilty of outrages, such as the sanctioning of the death penalty for political reasons (261).

Spain, known mainly for its jurists, missionaries, and soldiers during the sixteenth and seventeenth centuries, felt upon reaching the 1700's that something was missing. Looking out her window to the rest of Europe, fascinated by what she saw, she dispatched envoys to bring back scientific, artistic, and literary ideas with which to update universities, industry, and government. And while Spain truly needed to incorporate all the new advances, equally important was the maintenance and appreciation of what she already possessed—her laws, her painters and sculptors, her writers, her architects. Instead, these riches were relegated to a back room, slowing appreciation of the work of geniuses like El Greco, Velázquez and Francisco de Vitoria. Equally damaging was the timing of Spain's outreach to Europe. The 1750's in Europe are for Maeztu tantamount to the beginning of the greatest confusion in modern civilization. It certainly was a time of upheaval, when men such as Kant, Rousseau, Adam Smith, Montesquieu, Newton, and Leibniz revolutionized every branch of human knowledge. Spain, looking for a guiding star, found instead an unstable world bent on change at a vertiginous pace.

The error lies in the casting aside of institutions and their corresponding ideals when new and untested ones were imported.

The ensuing material disappointment though great could not
compare to the spiritual disillusionment that the exchange of foreign
ideals for traditionally national ones netted Spain. Most of it, Maeztu
believed, stemmed from the loss of a Christian legislative code and
the adoption of laws determined by the will of a ruler. Without these,
the very basis of moral jurisprudence was lost and so, too, was the
ecumenical tradition of every Hispanic country. When they seek
anew to regain their true national identity, these nations will find that
their historical sense is a universalizing one. Maeztu understood the
existence of a being as its *defense*. Spain's essential nature implies a
declared conviction, dating from the Council of Trent, that men
everywhere are morally equal. Being herself means Spain's defending herself, declares Maeztu, thereby upholding her traditional,
historical, and ecumenical role of imparting the ideals of Catholicism
and Spanish civilization, Hispanism. Consequent with the decline of
Spain and Spanish America, due to an eighteenth-century "suspicion of temporal superiority in other nations, contrary to our
[Catholic] faith" (286), there came a "deficiency" in Spain's creative
enterprises which, in circular fashion, only seemed to nurture the
feeling of inferiority. Now that the pendulum has swung the other
way, Spain by espousing her true historical role can be sure that the
values she once defended are the only true ones capable of ensuring
that her mission in the world can be accomplished. For Maeztu,
Spain's future lies in her past and Hispanism, being the most essential
part of that past, can best chart the course for the future.

V   *The Knights of Hispanism*

Maeztu believes in fertilization by the sediments of civilizations.
Using Italy as an example, he writes that the ruins of the Roman
empire served to inspire the Renaissance and, in turn, these
contributed to the rise of modern Italy under the dictatorship of
Benito Mussolini. From his visit there in April and May of 1924 he
came away convinced that under Mussolini's fascist rule the country
was on its way to becoming one of the power centers of the world. In
the same way he hoped that the cathedrals, palaces, and monasteries
built by Spain in the New World would have a similar effect on the
natives of these Spanish-American countries. That some day a native
Indian, and subsequently many, may come to find a deeper meaning
in the old stones and realize that Spain's work is yet to be finished is
not a chimera for Maeztu.

On the contrary, he is confident that one day Spain's work will inspire these people to take up the interrupted labor and fulfill their own destiny as the new knights of Hispanism. "Hispanism in history is nothing but an empire of faith" (293), he writes, further drawing the parallel between Rome and Spain. The lapse in the latter's case was due to the loss of faith when the Church was dislodged from its position as co-ruler with the country's monarchy. This loss, Maeztu has consistently argued, carried with it the loss of Spain's national ideal, so that indifference and indolence inexorably followed. But Spain's mission has only been interrupted; hers was a historical disorientation that can and must be rectified because her traditional ideal remained, in Maeztu's opinion, as the highest in the history of the world: to teach the whole of mankind that men are equal and thus capable of attaining eternal salvation. A Catholic monarchy is what Maeztu asked for the Spain of his day, with the same goals she proclaimed in her Golden Age: service to God, country, and king; hierarchy of principles and discipline; and brotherhood among all men. These, he carefully notes, would be the effective antagonists of the revolutionary motto "Liberty, Equality, Fraternity," which had done so much to undermine the concept of Hispanism.

In this longest of his books, rambling and repetitive at times as befits a collection of several dozen essays independently written and published, one main idea stands out—the need to unite Spain's temporal and religious powers to repeat her successes of the past. The many ideas that surface under different guises throughout the book can be summarized thus: 1) the continuing importance of Spain's messianic work, 2) the rejection of influences from abroad, 3) a return to the ideals of the sixteenth and seventeenth centuries, 4) the waging of war against both communism and capitalism, 5) the fight against revolution and in favor of a Catholic monarchy, 6) the proclamation of spiritual equality among men and their ability to achieve eternal salvation, 7) the notion that progress means adherence to the Christian faith, and 8) the defense of the work begun by Spaniards in the New World. For many, Maeztu's program amounted to nothing less than a fascist form of government and a rigidly orthodox Catholicism.[11] To others it smacked of archaic idealism, a utopia of the past without rational foundation.[12] Most consider it an impractical theopolitical system. Its idealistic patriotism and Catholic fervor no doubt preclude its viability at a time when international policy is dictated by the nuclear capabilities of those two nemeses Maeztu cautioned against, the United States and Russia.

CHAPTER 7

Miscellaneous Works and Summary

I Creative Writing

NOTHING has been said in the course of this book regarding
Ramiro de Maeztu's works of fiction. He did write poetry, some
drama, and one novel. None of these genres, however, show the
writer at his best or even at an adequate level of competency. His first
venture into literary creation takes the form of poetical composition.
An entire volume, written in the romantic vein of Espronceda and
still unpublished, was done in the years 1888–1890.[1] He continued,
during the first period of his residency in Madrid, to compose poems
of doubtful aesthetic worth. It was through the influence of Jacinto
Benavente that the weekly *Germinal*, a journal the dramatist
directed, accepted poems of Maeztu's, sometimes erotic ("Venus
gigantesca," "Gigantic Venus"), sometimes realistic ("Pescadores de
Sardinas," "Sardine Fishermen"). In the same magazine he was able
to place several short stories.[2] The social goal apparent in the last
poem cited appears also in what was to be Maeztu's first and last
dramatic piece, *El sindicato de las esmeraldas (The Emerald Guild)*,
written in 1908. In a letter to the writer Rojas, dated March 3, 1908,
Maeztu declared his intention of producing more plays, a theatrical
series: "I want to write an optimistic and realistic drama."[3] Nothing
came of it, however, since no further mention was ever heard about
the project. His largest work of fiction is a novel which appeared in
serialized installments, from April 1, 1900, to January 6, 1901.
Published for the first time in book form as recently as 1974, *La
guerra del Transvaal y los misterios de la Banca de Londres (The
Transvaal War and the Mysteries of London's Banks)* is a six-
hundred-page account of political, financial, and sociological plotting

in London, Johannesburg, Kimberly, and other distant places at the time of the war in South Africa. There are diamonds, gold, intrigue, and love besides, all with an eye to appeal to the widest possible reading public of the Madrid daily *El País*. That Maeztu was neither too sure nor too proud of the novel's literary worth is confirmed by the pseudonym artfully fabricated prior to the appearance of the work itself in the pages of *El País*. Van Poel Krupp, a Dutch newspaper correspondent and adventurer, with first-hand knowledge of the Transvaal conflict, serves as the mask behind which the real author perpetrated this literary hoax.[4]

Maeztu soon pushed aside literature per se, driving toward the ideological essay that became his lifetime standard. He was interested initially in industrial progress, economics, labor problems, technical advances; the rest he dismissed as literary opium. The series of autobiographical articles written between 1904 and 1908, though late, best represent the bridge which closes the gap between Maeztu's fiction and nonfiction. Certainly from the second date on, the nearest he came to engaging in any sort of purely literary enterprise was criticism, at times horribly off the mark (e.g., naming *Poniente Solar* [*Solar Dusk*] by Manuel Bueno as *the* novel of the Generation of 1898) and at others dissenting from traditionally held views as seen above in Chapter Five (*Don Quijote, Don Juan and Celestina*). Maeztu's path was to be *praxis* not *poyesis*.

II Lectures and Single Essays

One of the marks of personal worth in turn-of-the-century Madrid was an individual's ability as an orator. Maeztu, who delivered almost as many speeches as he wrote articles, was soon in great demand as a speaker. These talks found their way into his daily newspaper contributions and became a part of some of the books discussed earlier. Among his most celebrated is the lecture at Madrid's Ateneo in 1900, proclaiming the *Quijote* as a symbol of Spain's decadence, a notion loudly rejected, but later fully developed in *Don Quijote, Don Juan y la Celestina* (1925). A lecture widely celebrated to the point that national newspapers reprinted its text and a banquet was given in the author's honor was "La revolución y los intelectuales" ("Revolution and the Intelligentsia"). Read at the Ateneo in December 1910, Maeztu, from his international perspective as foreign correspondent, exhorted his audience to the Puritan ethic of work and austerity as a measure to revitalize Spain. Toward the end of his life, Maeztu's speeches reflect a deeply moral and conservative spirit. His entrance address before the Real Academia de Ciencias Morales y Políticas, entitled "El arte y la moral" ("Art and Ethics"), eschews the concept of art for art's sake as lacking true worth, saying that it resembles a snake biting its own tail. Maeztu judges art through life's looking glass.[5] The moral import of what probably would be his last significant public address is revealed by its title: "Sobre la brevedad de la vida en nuestra poesía lírica" ("On Life's Brevity in Our [Spanish] Lyric Poetry"), delivered upon his initiation into the Real Academia Española de la Lengua, Spain's most prestigious (and conservative) official literary organization.

Although many of Maeztu's essays have found their way into one book or another, two which have not been examined singly merit small mention at this juncture because of their constant presence in references to the writer. The first is "El sentido reverencial del dinero" ("The Reverence of Money"), a piece misunderstood by nearly all of his critics[6] and the subject of nearly a year's controversy (1926) in newspaper columns in Madrid and Buenos Aires.[7] Maeztu did not consider the ideal of making money as materialistic. Materialism in his eyes was thinking of wealth only in terms of the pleasures and comforts it can provide, but he did not advocate the cult of Mammom. Wealth for Maeztu was linked to a social function—a man who has been able to put together a fortune, by multiplying his money, will help others make money as well. This is something infinitely preferable to charity.[8] Thus Maeztu's reverence for money pertains to a sense of dedication to one's life and work. He vaguely echoes Adam Smith who cautioned that one must not hope to get the needed stuffs from the benevolence of the baker, the butcher, or the milkman, but instead as a result of their greed for making money.

The second essay, "Razones de una conversión" ("The Reasons Behind a Conversion"), was originally titled "Por qué me hice más católico" ("Why I Became More Catholic") but an unauthorized editor, much to Maeztu's annoyance, changed it.[9] Again, it was a case of misunderstanding, though so intriguing that it has given rise to dozens of articles and even served as the basis for a doctoral dissertation.[10] Written in 1934, this essay does not admit to any deviation from his Catholic upbringing. It traces rather the maturation and the intensification of that faith through his experiences in the First World War, his contacts with T. E. Hulme, the reading of Kant, Vitoria, González Arintero, and his ultimate conviction that his country's way in the sixteenth and seventeenth centuries had been the road to God. In other words, "The Reasons Behind a Conversion" recounts the factors which led Maeztu closer to his religion and why he believed it would prevail.

In these essays and nearly all that he wrote, Maeztu introduced a moral; his mind was oriented to "the way things should be."[11] Just as doctrinal were the last of his pieces which were to appear in the counterrevolutionary journal *Acción Española*, a publication he co-founded with the financial backing of the Marquis de Quintanar and the Marquis de Pelayo, two staunchly reactionary noblemen. Its first number, issued on December 16, 1931, contained an editorial by Maeztu himself that was to win the annual "Luca de Tena" journalistic award for that year.

III *Summary*

Maeztu's work has much in it that is "topical, hasty and obsolete" as befits a journalistic career spanning almost forty years,[12] and his books contain a certain amount of that eclecticism overloaded with polemics.[13] His writings attacked everyone and everything just as in daily life he argued in the street (his quick exit to London in 1905 was the result of a cane broken over a critic's head) and in the theater (he intended to carry a revolver to the premiere of Galdos' *Electra* and was challenged to a duel by Azorín afterwards). Maeztu considered philosophy not only a way of thinking, but of living, and did not distinguish between the two. His importance as an author lies in his thought and in the influence that it may have had on his contemporaries, much less in the purely aesthetic dimension of his writings.[14]

Maeztu's journalism was of a critical and reflective nature. A man of strong convictions, he was a totally humorless writer, passionate, patriotic, and intent on shaking his readers out of their social, political, and economic complacency. His work is neither rigorous nor scholarly, and his concern for stylistic and structural values is almost nil; his one goal appears to be preaching a doctrine and ensuring its impact in the mind of the reader.[15] Maeztu was one of the few newspapermen ever to think that journalism, far from being a step to some other position, represented a respectable profession worthy of a lifelong dedication; save for the brief stint as ambassador to Argentina, he never did anything other than write for a living. His audience being a heterogeneous group, Maeztu strove in his daily column for an approach to current topics somewhere between the elegant and the familiar. His style, at times ironic or even downright sarcastic, is penetrating, clear, vigorous, and eloquent. This last attribute on occasion produces long, involved sentences and rambling paragraphs where ideas fight for hegemony and the reader must thread his way with undivided attention.

Maeztu's mind was more receptive than it was creative of original thoughts. This is borne out when scrutinizing the evolution of his ideology. His initial residence in Madrid evinced no single heartfelt ideology, but following a period in London we see in him a liberal Socialist. After his trip to Marburg, Germany, he became a philosophically convinced Christian. His stay in the United States made him an admirer of its economic system; the years spent in contact with the dictatorship made him a fervent traditionalist, and the stay in Buenos Aires inspired the philosophy of Hispanism and convinced him of the government's and the Church's supreme roles. His last years were spent preparing the way for fascism in Spain. Three stages can be distinguished in this seemingly radical, ideological evolution ranging from anarchism to reactionary fascism.

The first stage, from 1891 until 1905, can be loosely described as his revolutionary period. It begins in Cuba where his social and unionist ideas germinated as he worked in sugar fields and tobacco factories. His readings at that time, which constituted part of his job (reading aloud to cigar makers), were Kipling, Schopenhauer, Kropotkin, Marx, and Sudermann—all revolutionary thinkers, the last of which impressed the young Maeztu so much that years later he prefaced a Spanish translation of the German philosopher's works. His first work reflects a destructive intent, doing away with the status quo, in contrast to the end of his life where he defends it with all his might. In both instances, however, he reacts to a given situation, either attacking it or defending it, rather than originating a completely new attitude. His writings appeared in all the major magazines and newspapers of the day. He was often the first of his generation to publish in the period's most influential publications, such as *El Imparcial*. What Maeztu wrote during those initial years is characterized by impatience and idealism. He rebelled against the duplicity of Spain's institutions, her bureaucrats, and her intellectuals. The fury with which he wrote exemplifies the faith he held for his country's future and, at the same time, urgency to implement the reforms called for in order to stave off utter chaos.

A liberal bordering on the romantic, his regenerationist stance cannot be doubted. One look at his lexicon ("toward another Spain," "a new Spain," "new people," "renovation," etc.) and the seriousness with which he resented Spain's backwardness compared with Europe, and his disdain for political practice attest to a genuine concern. His social awareness made him scorn intellectuals for not having provided an ideal for the country; the military, for their heroic view of Spain's place in the world; news media, for irresponsible reporting; and the general public for the negligence and abandon with which they slighted their obligations as citizens. This early revolutionary posture included a disapproving attitude toward the Church, which he considered a social institution with corresponding obligations toward society which he then felt it did not fulfill. In this first stage, the Nietzschean ideal of strong individualism pervades most of Maeztu's thought. His morality is that of the strong individual from which Spain's regeneration could derive. This amorality, his Europeanizing attitude, and the antigovernment stance will slowly evolve into equally intransigent but diametrically opposite beliefs by the time Maeztu succumbs in 1936.

Beginning in 1905, in the British capital, where he was to remain for a period of fifteen years, Maeztu's personality became more defined, and his clear journalist aptitudes matured noticeably. Gradually the stridency and combativeness of his initial output disappeared. Here, away from the constant bustle of Madrid and its café life Maeztu knew so intimately, he found ample time to write, study, and think at his own pace. The estrangement felt in London allowed him an opportunity to plot his future course. An ambitious man, he delved into the study of the classics and philosophy, and began to collaborate in some English journals such as *The New Age*, the official organ of the unionist movement in Britain. Its editor, A. R. Orage, and other contributors to the magazine had an impact on his sociopolitical ideas, already disposed toward a humanitarian socialism, and reinforced a "growing faith in the collective work of peoples, in the virtues of ideas and science."[16] To some of his enemies this gave the opportunity to charge that his Catholic upbringing had been overcome by a Protestant outlook, an accusation apparently substantiated by Maeztu's judgment that his stay in that country was the most important event of his life, an exaggeration perhaps not out of character of him.

The London years (1905–1919) proved to be most significant in the definitive makeup of his intellectual convictions. His fondness for Kant led him to the University of Marburg, Germany, held then as the Mecca of "philosophic rationalism."[17] The lessons of Nicolai Hartmann and Hermann Cohen on neo-Kantian philosophy awakened in him the need to believe in the existence of a spirit or soul as an entity totally separate from man's temporal self. Such a realization constituted the basis for a future religious thought steeped in traditional Catholic orthodoxy. From 1913 to 1916, Maeztu underwent an ideological crisis that turned him one hundred and eighty degrees. It was primarily of a religious nature, but consequent sociopolitical repercussions followed. Initially intellectual, its ultimate result was emotional, for it sparked the ideal of Hispanism, a union between Church and State, Catholicism and monarchy. [18]

The outbreak of World War I in the summer of 1914 shocked Maeztu and impelled him to see further the desirability of a morally controlled State. The preachings of T. E. Hulme regarding the objectivity of good vis à vis the relativism ascribed to it by modern man, and the exemplary conduct of this thinker did the rest. "Kant no basta" ("Kant isn't enough") was the title of an article written toward the end of the war where Maeztu argued that reason does not suffice to lead man to happiness. Though Kant serves as an initial stimulus, he does not provide enough hope, and so the arguments of other less rigorous philosophers such as the Thomistic Jacques Maritain become his new crutch.

The third and last stage of Maeztu's active public life begins upon his return to Spain in 1919. The country was in a crisis situation not altogether dissimilar to the one fifteen years earlier, and perhaps graver, with industrial strikes, regional separatist movements, economic downturn, political instability, public loss of confidence. If the situation paralleled the one he had left in 1905, however, Maeztu did not resemble his younger self, revealing a tenacious, conservative, religious spirit no longer skeptical about the compatibility of faith, culture, and progress. In fact it soon became evident that Maeztu's new conservatism did not allow for any of his earlier and others' present liberal convictions to meet on any issue or topic. Clearly his ideal was a Catholic, monarchical regime where people could have a reasonable input, a voice, though without returning to organized political parties or even a parliamentary system which he considered too divisive, ineffectual, and wasteful. His early defense of and subsequent identification with the dictatorship cost him dearly. The ire of the country's intellectuals, who opposed Primo de Rivera from the very beginning, descended on him as the most visible target of the counterrevolution. Ultimately, the archconservative *ABC* and his own *Acción Española* were the only major publications that carried his reactionary columns.

Whereas during Primo de Rivera's seven-year tenure not one political execution took place, the first months of the Second Republic were filled with crimes of every sort, looting, burning, and chaos. Maeztu continued to defend orthodoxy and authority, but those on the Right offered no support, while those on the Left waited for the opportune moment in which to silence him. His fervent Catholicism merited him the reputation of a blind moralist reactionary. Maeztu believed that one of the most significant causes for contemporary decadence was the lack of religious convictions,[19] dismissing as worthless a trust in man himself, in material progress, and technological advancement.[20] Having once thought that Europe was the solution to all Spain's problems, Maeztu now turned back to the sixteenth and seventeenth centuries when the country operated under an "ecumenical humanism"[21] intent on the spread of Christian values under the authority of a monarchical regime.

From 1934 on, everything Maeztu wrote became more and more a defense and a justification of his behavior, beliefs, and political convictions. His religious interpretation of history plus this defensive attitude first produced *In Defense of Hispanism*. The same religious conditioning of his political and philosophical views later prompted a second tome similarly inspired. A letter to a friend states that "I'm at work on a *Defensa del Espíritu (In Defense of the Spirit)* that is currently appearing in article form in the magazine *Acción Española,* and that I hope will make a pair with *In Defense of Hispanism.* Afterwards I would like to do another book on *Defensa de la Monarquía (In Defense of the Monarchy)* as protector of justice and Christian freedom. In this way my books will correspond to the terms of the old and traditional Spanish motto: God, Country and King."[22] Though published in 1958, the book is unfinished since Maeztu wrote the last chapters while awaiting his death in the Madrid prison, and they were confiscated. But its fragmented version speaks eloquently enough of its author's key point: We Spaniards have abandoned our religion and have nothing to put in its place.[23] It contains the same message found in the earlier *Defense,* the backward look at Spain's age of splendor in history, her Golden Age.

That Maeztu wished to write a third volume *In Defense of the Monarchy* is no surprise when one considers the backing he lent Primo de Rivera's dictatorship, a surrogate of the hoped-for monarchy. Death prevented him from going ahead with the project, and yet its unwritten pages pose no secret. Maeztu wanted a corporate state closely allied with the Catholic Church—ironically, for nearly forty years Franco's dictatorship provided just that. It was not exactly what Maeztu would have wanted, since he could not have sanctioned the longevity of such illegitimate authoritarianism, though it is equally difficult to see how he would have approved of the democratic bent of King Juan Carlos' liberal monarchy.

Notes and References

Chapter One

1. Hugh Thomas, *The Spanish Civil War* (New York, 1961), p. 209.
2. Luis Granjel, *La generación literaria del 98* (Salamanca, 1971), p. 192.
3. Ibid., p. 221.
4. Gonzalo Fernández de la Mora, "Maeztu y la noción de Humanidad," *Cuadernos Hispanoamericanos*, 33–34 (September–October, 1952), 77.
5. Vicente Marrero, *Maeztu* (Madrid, 1955), p. 160.
6. Cited by Granjel, op. cit., p. 164.
7. Cited by Marrero, op. cit., p. 159.
8. Ibid., p. 720.
9. Marrero, op. cit., p. 715.
10. Paul Ilie, "Nietzsche in Spain: 1890–1910," *PMLA*, 79 (March 1964), 80.
11. Gonzalo Sobejano, *Nietzsche en España* (Madrid, 1967), p. 60.
12. Marrero, op. cit., p. 260.
13. Azorín, *La Generación del 98* (Salamanca, 1969), p. 50.
14. Ibid., p. 91.
15. Sobejano, op. cit., p. 336.
16. Ibid., p. 510.
17. Azorín, op. cit., pp. 115–117.
18. Sobejano, op. cit., pp. 278 ff.
19. Ibid., p. 311.

Chapter Two

1. Marrero, op. cit., p. 14.
2. Ramiro de Maeztu, "Juventud menguante," *Cuadernos Hispanoamericanos*, 33–34 (September–October, 1952), 186.
3. Marrero, op. cit., p. 51.
4. Martin Nozick, "An Examination of Ramiro de Maeztu," *PMLA*, 69 (September 1954), 720.
5. Pío Baroja cited by Marrero, op. cit., p. 191.
6. Marrero, op. cit., p. 198.

7. María de Maeztu cited by Marrero, op. cit., p. 208.

8. Marrero, op. cit., p. 205.

9. María de Maeztu, *Antología—Siglo XX* (Madrid, 1943), p. 53.

10. Marrero, op. cit., p. 87.

11. Nozick, op. cit., p. 723.

12. Granjel, op. cit., p. 224.

13. Marrero, op. cit., pp. 294–295.

14. Enrique Tierno Galván, "El fundamento inconmovible del pensamiento de Ramiro de Maeztu," *Cuadernos Hispanoamericanos,* 33–34 (September–October 1952), 130–135.

15. Ibid., pp. 134–135.

16. Nozick, op. cit., p. 723.

17. Michael Roberts, *T. E. Hulme* (London, 1938), p. 35.

18. Alun Jones, *The Life and Opinions of T. E. Hulme* (Boston, 1960), p. 15.

19. Marrero, op. cit., p. 387.

20. Eugenio Vegas Latapié, "Evocación," *Defensa de la Hispanidad* (Madrid, 1934), p. xv.

21. Marrero, op. cit., p. 395.

22. For a more complete background on the subject see my primary source: Thomas, op. cit., pp. 64–73.

23. Ibid., p. 353.

24. Alberto Sánchez, "Introducción," *Don Quijote o el amor* (Salamanca, 1969), p. 27.

25. Thomas, op. cit., p. 173.

26. Marrero, op. cit., p. 731.

27. This is the most accepted version of Maeztu's death, though no one is sure whether he was executed inside the Ventas Prison or on the outskirts of Madrid.

Chapter Three

1. Carlos Blanco Aguinaga, *Juventud del 98* (Madrid, 1970), p. 174.

2. Will Durant, *The Story of Philosophy* (New York, 1961), p. 28.

3. Blanco Aguinaga, op. cit., p. 173.

4. Ramiro de Maeztu, *Hacia otra España* (Madrid, 1967), p. 120.

5. Ibid., p. 121.

6. Cited by Blanco Aguinaga, op. cit., p. 35.

7. Nozick, op. cit., p. 722.

8. Marrero, op. cit., p. 107.

Chapter Four

1. All subsequent page references are to the 1949 edition of *La crisis del Humanismo.*

2. Julán Marías, *Historia de la filosofía* (Madrid, 1967), p. 316.

3. Durant, op. cit., p. 226.
4. José Oretga y Gasset, *La deshumanización del arte* (Madrid, 1925).
5. José Ortega y Gasset, *La rebelión de las masas* (Madrid, 1930).
6. Marrero, op. cit., p. 340.

Chapter Five

1. Cited by A. Sánchez, op. cit., p. 37.
2. Marrero, op. cit., p. 430.
3. Sobejano, op. cit., p. 342.
4. Alberto Porqueras Mayo, *Temas y formas de la literatura española* (Madrid, 1972), p. 143. See the bibliographical entry for this author. The same essay appears under two entries.
5. Sobejano, op. cit., p. 334.
6. Cited by A. Sánchez, op. cit., p. 67.
7. *Ibid.*, p. 48.
8. All subsequent page references are to *Don Quijote, Don Juan y La Celestina* (Espasa-Calpe Argentina, 1952).
9. Sobejano, op. cit., p. 343.
10. David W. Foster, "Some Attitudes Towards Love in the *Celestina*," *Hispania*, 48 (September, 1965), 484.
11. Denis de Rougemont, *Love in the Western World* (New York, 1965),
12. Ibid., p. 15.

Chapter Six

1. Anon, "Ramiro de Maeztu," *ABC*, 2 September 1952, p. 1.
2. María de Maeztu, op. cit., p. 57.
3. Angel Valbuena Prat, *Historia de la literatura española*, III (Barcelona, 1950), p. 501.
4. Ibid., p. 501.
5. Robert Bancroft, "América en la obra de Ramiro de Maeztu," *Revista Hispánica Moderna*, 13 (July–October, 1947), 248.
6. The word *hispanidad*, although used by others such as Unamuno, had been deemphasized by the Spanish Royal Academy of Language as archaic. It was thanks to Maeztu that, from the 1939 edition of the dictionary of the Academy on, *hispanidad* was defined as "carácter genérico de todos los pueblos de lengua y cultura españolas" ("generic character of all the nations of Spanish language and culture").
7. All subsequent page references are from the third edition (Valladolid, 1938) of *Defensa de la Hispanidad*.
8. José Pemartín, "El pensamiento político de Maeztu posterior a *La crisis del humanismo*," *Cuadernos Hispanoamericanos*, 33–34 (September–October, 1952), 189–190.

9. Ibid., pp. 88–89.
10. Ibid., p. 89.
11. Nozick, op. cit., p. 734.
12. Sobejano, op. cit., p. 346.

Chapter Seven

1. Maeztu, "El monumento a Espronceda," *Cuadernos Hispanoamericanos*, 33–34 (September–October, 1952), 189–190.
2. The two poems were published on August 13 and July 23, 1897, respectively. That same year Maeztu published the following short stories: "Central consueño" (July 23), "El hijo muerto (Redimidos)" (July 30), "Alma cifra" (August 20), "El triunfo de un cobarde" (September 24), "Mujer de su casa" (October 1), "Deportado" (October 8), "Desdoblamiento" (October 9), and "Fiebre y vòmito" (October 10). All except the penultimate story, from the magazine *Vida Nueva*, appeared in *Germinal*. For a further elaboration of this facet of Maeztu consult my source: Luis S. Granjel, *Baroja y otras figuras del 98* (Madrid, 1960), pp. 155–176.
3. Ricardo Rojas, *El retablo español* (Buenos Aires, 1938), p. 253.
4. See E. Inman Fox's fascinating prologue to the work *La guerra del Transvaal y los misterios de la Banca de Londres* (Madrid, 1974), pp. 9–20.
5. Marrero, op. cit., p. 727.
6. A notable exception is Enrique Fernández Barros, "Don Ramiro de Maeztu y el sentido del dinero en la vida norteamericana," *Revista de Estudios Hispánicos*, 10 (October 1976), 323–344.
7. Maeztu, "La riqueza norteamericana. El ideal de Igualdad y Libertad," *La Prensa*, 14 November 1926. Quoted by Pemartín, op. cit., p. 95.
8. Marrero, op. cit., p. 501.
9. Eugenio Vegas, "Maeztu y *Acción Española*, *ABC*, 2 November 1952.
10. Rafael V. Martínez, "La conversión de Ramiro de Maeztu." Unpublished Ph.D. Diss. (Northwestern University, 1964). See the bibliography on the subject provided at the end of this work.
11. Gonzalo Fernández de la Mora, "Maeztu y la teoría de la Revolución," in Maeztu's *Frente a la República* (Madrid, 1956), p. 11.
12. Nozick, op. cit., p. 719.
13. Porqueras, op. cit., p. 147.
14. Gonzalo Torrente Ballester, *Panorama de la literatura española contemporánea* (Madrid, 1956), p. 225.
15. Emiliano Díez–Echarri y José María Roca Franquesa, *Historia de la literatura española e hispanoamericana* (Madrid, 1960), p. 1271.
16. Sobejano, op. cit., p. 326.
17. Martínez, op. cit., p. 87.
18. Ibid., p. 127.
19. Marrero, op. cit., p. 416.

20. Nozick, op. cit., p. 737.
21. Sobejano, op. cit., p. 326.
22. Sánchez, op. cit., p. 26.
23. Marrero, op. cit., p. 661.

Selected Bibliography

PRIMARY SOURCES

Most of Maeztu's work, between thirteen and fifteen thousand newspaper articles and essays, appeared in various periodicals, many now defunct. Due to the enormous size of his production and the consequent difficulty in cataloguing (plus the obviously uneven quality inherent in so much writing), I have not attempted a total compilation. Instead I have chosen to list only those of Maeztu's works published in book form. The reader wishing a more complete reference regarding the author's periodical publications is advised to consult the following sources: Ano. "Artículos de Ramiro de Maeztu publicados en *ABC*." *ABC*, 2 November, 1952 [2 unnumbered pages]; Fox, E. Inman. "Una bibliografía anotada del periodismo de Ramiro de Maeztu y Whitney (1897-1904)." *Cuadernos Hispanoamericanos*, 291 (September, 1974), 528-581; Gamallo Fierros, Dionisio. "Hacia un Maeztu total." *Cuadernos Hispanoamericanos*, 33-34 (September-October, 1952), 279-496; also by this same critic, under the same title and in the same journal, Vol. 39 (March, 1953), 26 unnumbered pages.

Hacia otra España. Bilbao: Biblioteca Vascongada de Fermín Herrán, 1899.

Debemos a Costa. El hombre y sus ideas. Zaragoza: N/p, 1911.

La revolución y los intelectuales. Madrid: Ateneo, 1911.

Authority, Liberty and Function in the Light of the War. London: George Allen & Unwin Ltd. New York: The Macmillan Co., 1916.

Inglaterra en armas. Una visita al frente. London: Darling & Son, Ltd., 1916.

La crisis del humanismo. Barcelona and Bilbao: Editorial Minerva, 1919.

Don Quijote, Don Juan y la Celestina. Madrid: Espasa-Calpe, 1925.

Defensa de la Hispanidad. Madrid: Fax, 1934.

La brevedad de la vida en nuestra poesía lírica. Madrid: Gráfica Universal, 1935.

En vísperas de la tragedia. Ed. José María de Areilza. Madrid: Cultura Española, 1941.

España y Europa. Ed. María de Maeztu. Madrid: Espasa-Calpe, 1947.

Ensayos. Ed. María de Maeztu. Buenos Aires: Emecé, 1948.

147

Frente a la República. Ed. Gonzalo Fernández de la Mora. Madrid: Rialp, 1956.

El sentido reverencial del dinero. Ed. Vicente Marrero. Madrid: Editora Nacional, 1957.

Liquidación de la monarquía parlamentaria. Ed. Vicente Marrero. Madrid: Editora Nacional, 1957.

Norteamérica desde dentro. Ed. Vicente Marrero. Madrid: Editora Nacional, 1957.

Con el Directorio Nacional. Ed. Vicente Marrero. Madrid: Editora Nacional, 1957.

Defensa del espíritu. Ed. Antonio Millán Puelles. Madrid: Rialp, 1958.

Las letras y la vida en la España de entreguerras. Ed. Vicente Marrero. Madrid: Editora Nacional, 1958.

El nuevo tradicionalismo y la revolución social. Ed. Vicente Marrero. Madrid: Editora Nacional, 1959.

Un ideal sindicalista. Ed. Vicente Marrero. Madrid: Editora Nacional, 1961.

Autobiografía. Ed. Vicente Marrero. Madrid: Editora Nacional, 1962.

Don Quijote o el Amor. Ed. Alberto Sánchez. Madrid Anaya, 1964.

Los intelectuales y un epílogo para estudiantes. Ed. Vicente Marrero. Madrid: Editora Nacional, 1966.

La guerra del Transvaal y los misterios de la Banca de Londres. Ed. E. Inman Fox. Madrid: Taurus, 1974.

Obra. Ed. Vicente Marrero. Madrid: Editora Nacional, 1974. Includes *Autobiografía, La crisis del humanismo, Don Quijote, Don Juan y la Celestina, El sentido reverencial del dinero, Defensa de la Hispanidad, Defensa del espíritu, El arte y la moral,* and *La brevedad de la vida en nuestra poesía lírica.*

Artículos periodísticos (1897-1905). Ed. E. Inman Fox. Madrid: Castalia, 1975.

SECONDARY SOURCES

AGUIRRE PRADO, LUIS. *Ramiro de Maeztu.* Madrid: EPESA, 1974. A sketchy, journalistic appraisal of Maeztu's life and main works. Devoid of critical value.

BANCROFT, ROBERT. "América en la obra de Ramiro de Maeztu." *Revista Hispánica Moderna,* 13 (July–October, 1947), 236–249. A narrated inventory of Maeztu's writings dealing with the Americas.

BESER, SERGIO. "Un artículo de Maeztu contra Azorín." *Bulletin Hispanique,* 55 (1963), 329–332. An account of the polemic between these two figures as a result of the premiere of Galdós' play *Electra* in January 1901.

BLANCO AGUINAGA, CARLOS. *Juventud del 98.* Madrid: Siglo Veintiuno, 1970. Enlightening examination of Maeztu's first years as a member of the Generation of 98. Good critical analysis of ideas contained in *Hacia otra España.*

DIAZ PLAJA, GUILLERMO. *Modernismo frente a Noventa y ocho.* Madrid: Espasa-Calpe, 1966. Classification of Maeztu as an ideologue of anti-aesthetic attitudes.

FERNANDEZ BARROS, ENRIQUE. "Pérez Galdós y Menéndez Pelayo en el pensamiento de Ramiro de Maeztu." *Abside,* 36 (1972), 193–200. Sees Maeztu as one of the first in challenging view of Galdós as "novelista del liberalismo español" to the detriment of literary values of his work. Clarifies Maeztu's ambivalent stance towards Menéndez Pelayo.

————. "Ramiro de Maeztu, un defensor del espíritu." *Abside,* 39 (1975), 273–309. A subjective, introductory, historico-biographical survey identifying the man and his work.

————. "Don Ramiro de Maeztu y el sentido del dinero en la vida norteamericana." *Revista de Estudios Hispánicos,* 10 (October 1976), 323–344. Lucid exposition of Maeztu's often misunderstood sociospiritual appraisal of money and wealth.

FOX, E. INMAN. "Galdós' *Electra:* A Detailed Study of its Historical Significance and the Polemic between Martínez Ruiz and Maeztu." *Anales Galdosianos,* 1 (1966), 131–141. Similar to Beser's above article on the same topic though more comprehensive.

————. "Ramiro de Maeztu y los intelectuales." *Revista de Occidente,* 51 (June 1967), 369–377. Maeztu's intellectual history succinctly delineated as to how it falls in importance just below Unamuno's and Ortega's.

————. "Una bibliografía anotada del periodismo de Ramiro de Maeztu y Whitney (1897–1904)." *Cuadernos Hispanoamericanos,* 291 (September, 1974), 528–581. A useful, detailed synthesis of more than four hundred journalistic pieces of Maeztu between the time he arrives in Madrid and his departure for London.

GAMALLO FIERROS, DIONISIO. "Un olvidado ciclo de conferencias de Maeztu en 1902." *Cuadernos Hispanoamericanos,* 291 (September, 1974), 481–527. A valuable summary of nine lectures given by Maeztu in the Galician city of Vigo, some of which became articles.

GOMEZ MARTINEZ, JOSE LUIS. "Ramiro de Maeztu: El hombre y su ideal." *Abside,* 38 (1974), 196–201. Summary of Maeztu's evolution in his desire to strengthen national individuality and identity.

GRANJEL, LUIS S. "Baroja, Azorín y Maeztu en las páginas de *El Pueblo Vasco.*" *Cuadernos Hispanoamericanos,* 109 (January, 1959), 5–17. The nature of the early writings of the group in the San Sebastián daily.

————. *La generación literaria del noventa y ocho.* Salamanca: Anaya, 1971. Interesting and fresh account of the Generation of 98 and its members until 1905 when, in the critic's opinion, Maeztu and the rest ceased to function as a group.

———. *Baroja y otras figuras del 98.* Madrid: Guadarrama, 1960. Maeztu's ideas around the time of the publication of his earliest book, biographically oriented.

LIDA, CLARA E. "Literatura anarquista y anarquismo literario." *Nueva Revista de Filología Hispánica,* 19 (1970), 360–381. Literary anarchism as a way of life at the turn of the century when Maeztu, Azorín, and Baroja became known.

MAEZTU, MARIA DE. *Antología—Siglo XX.* Madrid: Espasa-Calpe, 1964. Of all the brief studies, in the form of prefaces and introductions to her brother's works, the essay included here is the most general and informative.

MARRERO SUAREZ, VICENTE. "En torno a la obra de Maeztu, a los dieciséis años después de su muerte." *Arbor,* 23 (December, 1952), 425–427. Personal lament at the lack of rigorous criticism of Maeztu, plus the announcement of two Festschrift (see following section).

———. *Maeztu.* Madrid: Rialp, 1955. The most comprehensive (756 pages) study of Maeztu's life and works. Written in an adulatory tone, the volume remains a useful source of valuable data of all kinds in spite of its drawbacks.

MARTINEZ, RAFAEL. "La conversión de Ramiro de Maeztu." Unpublished Doctoral Dissertation. Northwestern University, 1964. Focuses on the changes of Maeztu's ideological convictions.

NOZICK, MARTIN. "An Examination of Ramiro de Maeztu." *Publications of the Modern Language Association,* 69 (September, 1954), 719–740. The first and to date the only major essay in English on Maeztu. Fortunately, it is also the best general critical appraisal of the author's thought. The most informative all-inclusive study on either Maeztu or his principal works.

ORTEGA Y GASSET, JOSE. "Sobre una apología de la exactitud." *Obras Completas,* Vol. I. Madrid: Revista de Occidente, 1953. Intellectual discrepancies between the two thinkers are here aired by Ortega.

PEREZ DE LA DEHESA, RAFAEL. *El pensamiento de Costa y su influencia en el 98.* Madrid: Sociedad de Estudios y Publicaciones, 1966. Tracing of the ideological debts of Maeztu to Costa, dating from 1899 to the former's London socialist period.

PORQUERAS MAYO, ALBERTO. "*El Quijote* en un rectángulo del pensamiento moderno español." *Revista Hispánica Moderna,* 28 (1962), 26–35. An intelligent article on Cervantes' masterpiece in the twentieth century. The section on Maeztu concentrates on his view of the *Quijote* as the book reflecting Spain's decline in the world.

RIO, EMILIO DEL. *La idea de Dios en la Generación del 98.* Madrid: Studium Ediciones, 1973. Emphasizes the uniqueness of Maeztu among the Generation of 98, the only man of action, the only one to escape doubt, the only one to die for his ideas.

ROCAMORA, PEDRO. "Ramiro de Maeztu v la Generacion del 98." *Arbor,*

341 (May, 1974), 7–22. A look at Maeztu's metamorphosis from a young radical into a mature Catholic reactionary.

SISTO, DAVID T. "A Note on the Philosophy of Ramiro de Maeztu and Carlos Reyles." *Hispania,* 41 (1958), 457–459. On the Nietzschean idealism held in common by the Uruguayan novelist and Maeztu.

SOBEJANO, GONZALO. *Nietzsche en España.* Madrid: Gredos, 1967. A formidable study of the German philosopher's impact on modern Spain's letters. Sobejano argues, not unconvincingly, for Maeztu's lifelong adherence to Nietzsche's philosophy of the Superman.

VAL, VENANCIO DEL, et al. *En torno a Ramiro de Maeztu.* Vitoria: Caja de Ahorros Municipal, 1974. Unable to consult this work firsthand. It warrants mention in this bibliography, though the publisher makes it suspect, because of the dearth of monographs.

ZULETA, EMILIA. *Historia de la crítica española contemporánea.* Madrid: Gredos, 1966. In the section dedicated to the Generation of 98, there is a brief but accurate and perceptive assessment of Maeztu's critical trajectory.

Special Numbers of Journals Devoted to Ramiro de Maeztu

"Homenaje a Don Ramiro de Maeztu." *ABC,* 2 November, 1952. Collaborations by friends and disciples, plus a bibliography of all of Maeztu's articles published in this newspaper.

"Homenaje a Ramiro de Maeztu." *Cuadernos Hispanoamericanos,* 33–34 (September–October, 1952). A five hundred page *Festschrift* of uneven but irreplaceable value in honor of Maeztu, written mostly by political figures of the Right. Personal pieces alternate with criticism of a literary or philosophic nature. Should be read with a grain of salt. Recommended are the essays by Tierno Galván, José Pemartín, Gonzalo Fernández de la Mora, and Dionisio Gamallo Fierros.

Index